MW00987395

LADIES, YOUR DATING PICKER IS BROKEN

8 Proven Steps for women to fix their Love and Dating List, pick a high-quality man, and have a healthy relationship!

VICTORIA KNIGHTLEY

contained within this document, including, but not limited to, errors, omissions, or inaccuracies.

Free Gift For My Readers!

A Relaxing Gratitude Journal to unwind while you find Mr. Right

90 Days of Positivity and Fun

Free additional printable pages for your gratitude practice!

Scan the QR code above with your smartphone or tablet

PREFACE

Hello, my lovelies,

To those of you who are discovering the Brilliant
Vixen for the first time, welcome! For all my existing
vixens, welcome back. Since the last time I wrote,
I've been thinking about the perfect follow-up to my
first book, "The 7 Essential Elements of Irresistible
Women", and then it hit me. Most of the lovely ladies
I meet are starting at a disadvantage because they're
looking for the wrong man from the moment they
begin. One truth in love is that if you look for the
wrong man, you'll most certainly find him.

So I craft this book out of necessity and an abun-
dance of affection for my lovely ladies. I've seen far

too many ladies in my life be understandably frustrated that they aren't finding love, and when I try to clear their minds and ask them what they are looking for, I'm usually met with confusion and "I just want a nice guy." Then there's a huge sigh followed by the requisite ice cream.

There are two components to meeting a new man.
1. Attraction- What are you putting out there? Which I covered with "The 7 Essential Elements of Irresistible Women"
2. Selection-What kind of guy are you picking?

I've heard a significant number of women use the phrase "my picker's broken," to them, I say my hats off to you, my dear. You're acknowledging that something isn't right, which is the first step. Clarity is not always easy to achieve, but it's the truth. It's been my tremendous pleasure to help bring the truth to your list in a way that will set you up for success.

This book has been meticulously crafted to help you create a list so powerful that you will know what will make you happy before you go on your next date.

Not only that, but you'll know if he's Mr. Wrong **on just one date!** I've developed a system based on a sound psychological foundation that will sniff out bad matches quickly, not wasting months or years of slow trial and error.

Time is our most precious asset, and this book is designed to protect it for you. Brilliant Vixen is about making dating a fun experience for you, my lovely ladies. Part of that fun is not stressing about how you're selecting your perfect match.

This book will give you a rock-solid new list to separate what will genuinely make you happy from what is holding you back. No, we're not talking about what would make your friends happy or what makes your frenemies from work happy. We're here to find what kind of guy would make you a beam-with-joy level of happy.

I've even included examples of dates that were...great stories, let's call them. Those who know me know that I categorize dates into two different boxes. They are either "great dates" or "great stories." These fall into the "great stories" box. I saw what I didn't want in a man during these dates. They also demonstrate how men can show their cards in one dimension so clearly that I knew we were incompatible on the spot. No second date was required. These were great learning experiences, and I'm sharing these with you lovely ladies so you can see how to use similar experiences to your advantage.

Brilliant Vixen is about developing a complete system for ladies who are serious about finding their forever Prince Charming. No, not the cookie-cutter one-dimensional cartoon kind, though! We're all about finding and attracting quality men interested in forever romance. This is the critical next book after my first book, "The 7 Essential Elements of Irresistible Women", focused on attracting men. Now with that knowledge in hand, we need a method to sort out the great matches from the not-so-great. That's why I needed to write this book next. Helping ladies have a powerful list based on well-being is perfect for our end goal here, which is genuine lasting love.

This book will help you put together a list that will help you choose a partner that is truly a match on all levels and will help you build a happy and healthy long-term relationship. Because, after all, if you don't even know what you want, then how will you find it? Or know when you've found it? This book will require a bit of work and introspection. If you feel that it is worth it to find a fulfilling relationship, then this is the book for you!

Adjusting your list is not settling, and I would never advocate for that in a million years. We're changing our aim for true happiness instead of ticking empty boxes that ultimately rob you of true love.

Let's look at where we're at now.

Current List Exercise: I don't know if you have an official list yet or if it's just an approximate idea floating in your subconscious. For our purposes, we're going to make a simple list to set a foundation for where we are today. Start with a list of 10 things you want in a man. These are just the first ten items that come to mind. This list is a primary starting point to see what currently comes to mind. Then a list of 5 deal breakers. Again this is just a starting point. We'll make sure your list evolves with each passing chapter.

Please don't put too much pressure on yourself to get it perfect, but don't move on to the next section without completing it either.

Ten things you want in a man
 aka "Must-Haves"
  1.
  2.
  3.

4.
5.
6.
7.
8.
9.
10.

5 things you absolutely won't tolerate in a romantic partner

aka "Deal-Breakers" or "Time-Savers."

1.
2.
3.
4.
5.

This is your list as it stands now. There are no judgments here about the current condition of your list. If this is the first time you've written it down, I am happy to be a part of it. If you've already had to pare down your list from 100 to just the top 15, that's also ok! Either way, we'll use this as a baseline to compare to as we move to the list that will give you the things you truly want and help you walk away quickly from the things you don't.

We're going to start by focusing on the positive "Must-Have" traits and leave the "Deal-Breakers" for the end. It's ok if some ideas on the subject pop up but let's try to start by just focusing on the positive qualities which would add emotional richness to our lives.

Each of our lists is different. Each is based on our life experiences; sometimes, those experiences are hurtful and leave us feeling unloved or broken. It's important that we craft our new list out of joyfulness and love and that we leave these negative emotions behind. You never forget the lessons you've learned but leave the harmful feelings aside while you craft your present moment. So for the remainder of this book, we'll stay in the present and not worry about any other time. A wise friend once shared a secret about staying in the moment that I'd like to share with you.

"To live in the past can lead to depression, to live in the future can lead to anxiety, and to live right now is perfection."

-Dr. Mark Anderson, Nevada Center for Behavioral Therapy

It's essential to stay in the moment to craft our new list with an open mind and heart. Do yourself a loving kindness and cast aside all societal pressure to make your list appeal to the masses. They won't be living this life for you. We're crafting a list that will bring you the love and joy you deeply deserve.

Here's the big secret to this book. This book will not only give you the tools to make your list powerful but also make you feel that power inside yourself. We will be taking a candid look at our actions and why.

This book is based on "The 8 Dimensions of Wellness," a concept Developed by Dr. Peggy Swarbrick. This concept is an intensely powerful and all-encompassing approach to living a happy life.

"Swarbrick developed her nationally recognized wellness model to help herself cope with severe mental illness that struck in adolescence. 'Initially,' she writes, this [wellness vision] kept me alive, and now it has helped me live each day more fully." -Mel Kobrin SAMHSA.gov

---

I chose to use the eight dimensions of wellness as a

framework. This framework addresses what makes a person thrive in all areas of life. I believe it is the perfect basis to use when searching for the ideal partner to share that life with. Applying the 8 Dimensions of Wellness to dating helps us leave no stone unturned. This will help to generate a feeling of peace in our dating adventure, knowing that we have all the bases covered while leaving room for incredible discovery.

"Wellness is an active process of becoming aware of and making choices toward a healthy and fulfilling life. Wellness is more than being free from illness; it is a dynamic process of change and growth. It is a state of complete physical, mental, and social well-being and not merely the absence of disease or infirmity." - Dr. Donald Ardell, Author "High-Level Wellness: An Alternative to Doctors, Drugs, and Disease"

Now that we've addressed the foundation for the book let's go one step further.

Before we do that, I just wanted to say thank you so much for all the heartwarming emails about how my work has affected your life. Fun, Flirty, Genuine,

High-Value, Challenge, Mystery, Constantly Evolving.
These are the "7 Essential Elements of Irresistible
Women". As discussed in my previous book, men
should also have these characteristics or the male
equivalent. All of these have been wildly successful
with fans of the first book. But that book still focuses
on attraction. Attraction is critical, but now we need
to build on that and focus on the type of man we
want to attract.

When assessing long-term compatibility, different
elements were more conducive to figuring out solid
and specific must-haves and deal-breakers. This is
different from how the dimensions of wellness are
typically laid out in other studies. For our purposes,
these dimensions of wellness are arranged to start
with what seems like the most surface dimensions
into the deeper, more profound dimensions, in which
true compatibility is revealed.

When I've asked many women what they like or want
in a man, I hear a growing number of problematic
responses. Usually something along the lines of, "I
want a guy at least 6 ft tall, who makes six figures, and
has six-pack abs."

Oh, love, I'm afraid that won't do at all, will it? You're
already sailing in the wrong direction, so it's no

wonder you keep repeatedly finding the wrong man. Those things are nice, but none of them speak to the kind of connection which will fill the remainder of your years with emotional richness and joy.

There are many times in our life when we need to work on our "Picker." When we're young, our picker is new and doesn't come pre-loaded with much information. As we grow, we need to recalibrate to reflect our changing priorities. Sometimes a particularly bad relationship can make us feel like it's broken altogether. We aren't broken, though. Just in need of some new information and a little recalibration!

Now it's time to make a list of the things you truly want in a man!

Brilliant Vixen Secret Bonus: Ok, ladies, it's time to look under your metaphorical chairs for your bonus to this book. (*Actually, the secret bonuses are at the end of every chapter!) I've designed a way for every one of these points to contain a new way to meet the perfect guy for you! We're diving deep into our well-being, and in that discovery, we're going to uncover some exciting ways to find Mr. Right!

*I suggest getting a pen and paper so you can make notes as you find your way through the sections of

this book. There are spaces throughout the book for
your potential new list items, but there are also many
activities and question sections where you would
benefit greatly from scribbling down some notes!

Now without further ado, let's begin making our new
list, shall we?

Chapter One

PHYSICAL

"It's your road and yours alone.
Others may walk it with you,
but no one can walk it for you." -Rumi.

Ok, this is easy, right? 6 feet tall and six-pack abs. Done. Next. Not even close, ladies. Although "physical" sounds like picking all the juicy bits in movies or magazines, like everything in this book, it goes so much deeper than that. We're going to look at the three areas that make up the critical part of the "physical" dimension and how most women aren't looking at this in a way that serves them best.

When we're looking at this from the angle of our wellness and happiness, then we should take a look at recognizing the need for physical activity, sleep, and diet/nutrition. So let's break that down one at a time to see how that relates to choosing a mate. Because knowing yourself and what truly brings you joy makes it so much easier to see what kind of mate would make you even happier! This is the first dimension to finding someone who can walk with us. That's why I selected the quote by Rumi to start this chapter.

Physical Activity: Determining your level of physical activity will help you match up with someone who shares a pace you enjoy. Simple enough as a concept. Now let's dig in deeper so we can define it more.

How often are you physically active (be honest!), and what kind of physical activity? Are you a 3x-a-week gym member? A weekend hiker? A leisurely stroll after dinner type of person? If you have a goal that you aren't currently working on but is important enough to you to start scheduling time for it in the next week, then write that down too.

If you currently only workout once a month, but your goal is 3x a week, then getting on track with your goals will help you find someone aligned with where you want to be. Many women I've talked to (and men as well!) have said they want a partner with "6-pack abs" or some other physical attribute that generally requires dedication to achieve, especially the older we get. Meanwhile, they are not similarly dedicated to those same goals.

It is also unfair to think that someone will come along and motivate you to achieve your goals. That is your responsibility, and if you need help (as we all sometimes do), then that is the job of a coach or trainer. Refrain from putting this pressure or expectation on a person you have yet to meet. A great partner will indeed be there to cheer you on to the finish line or maybe run by your side, but you must already be in the race.

Now maybe what you really want is someone who will snuggle with you on the couch all weekend while drinking hot cocoa with an absolutely ridiculous amount of mini marshmallows in it. Once again, no judgment! If a cuddly slow-paced weekend staying in and watching movies is your jam, then do the heck out of that. Just make sure that what you're looking for physically in a man lines up with the level of activity you also want to do. In the end, if you aren't invested in the same kind of activities, then it becomes increasingly difficult to enjoy spending time together.

Now, none of this means that you can't have both! Or neither! Every variation of human exists on this planet. It just means that you need to take a look at what a life together would look like long term.

This is a great moment to take inventory of how much physical activity you enjoy and change it if it needs to be aligned with your true self. Or accept and love it if it is your true self, but you feel judged by the outside world for it. Loving yourself makes it much easier to find and accept love outside of yourself.

Sleep- I adore my precious sleep. Your relationship with sleep is incredibly important, and your ideal partner's relationship with sleep is equally important. Let's look at this in the context of dating.

If you're a night owl and you meet someone who starts their day by running at 5 am every day and goes to bed at 9 pm, how exactly are you going to spend time together? I used to date a musician who worked until the wee hours of the morning and would crash out just as I was getting up for my day. Rinse and repeat over a year, and it was unsustainable. This is not to say that your schedules have to be perfectly aligned, just compatible enough that you can comfortably spend time together.

Do you have a night job or an early morning start time? Do you like to stay up late drinking, rise early to bird watch, or get a run-in? Quite often, our wake and sleep schedules actually say quite a bit more than we realize about our priorities. Write down your current schedule and if it isn't what truly makes you happy, then write down what would make you more comfortable. As we craft our list, it's the perfect time to change our lives. If those changes align with your true self, your new love will feel like a validating reward for your new choices.

An exciting part about this one is that it might be apparent from the moment you try to organize a date.

Him: I'd love to take you to dinner on Friday night. Does that sound good?
You: I work this weekend. What about Monday? Dinner then?
Him: Oh, I can't. I have to be up really early Monday through Friday.

Just scheduling this first date will tell you loads about their schedule. As you can see from this example, it's already rough scheduling a first date. It's not the end of the world if scheduling your first date is tricky, but pay attention to it.

Diet/Nutrition -Be brutally honest with yourself. No one else needs to ever see this! Write down what an average day of meals looks like for you. Fast food? Home-cooked meals? Fancy restaurants? All organic, vegan, vegetarian, raw or some other specific and regimented dietary plan?

Are you happy with what you're eating? If yes, then YAY! If not, then do you remember a time when you were happier? Do you have a plan that would make you feel more vibrant? As long as what you eat makes you feel good, you won't hear another peep from me. I want to ensure your fuel adds to your well-being, not takes away from it.

Again, this is not about judgment about what makes you happy! Only you know what makes your soul do a happy dance! My giant construction worker of a brother finds his happy place with a 32 oz cold soda and a chili cheese dog from a convenience store. That is seriously his jam! Because of this I wouldn't recommend a vegan foodie as a life match for him. Neither of them would be happy when mealtimes came around, and food is a pretty integral part of day-today life. That doesn't mean everything has to be an exact match, though. It turns out he's pretty happy with home-cooked chili, which is certainly healthier than its gas station counterpart but it doesn't kill the joy in his big ole heart.

We've all heard the phrase opposites attract. Well, that doesn't work when you look at each other's plate in horror across the dinner table. You can be different, and in fact, discovering new cuisines and recipes is a whole lot of fun. I love trying out new restaurants and cookbooks, and I'm still constantly finding new favorites. With that being said, wildly conflicting food ideologies make sharing something as necessary as eating several times a day difficult.

This is another dimension you can figure out before the first date starts. When you're looking to set up the first date, you're going to discuss what kind of food you like to eat. In your banter, he will most likely ask you what your favorite type of food is. That's fantastic, but instead of just answering straight away, give him your top 3 styles of cuisine and ask him what his top 3 are. That way, you can see a pattern, not just him agreeing to go to a restaurant because he wants to take you on a date.

Now you might be looking at this section and saying,

"But where's the part where I write down that he needs to be tall, dark and handsome?" Ok, I understand there are physical traits that we find attractive, but if your perfect match is on a dating app and they have brown eyes instead of blue, and it doesn't fit your criteria, by one click, you may have done yourself a great disservice.

We'll make a deal here; when you get to the end of this chapter, you can write down a maximum of two purely physical characteristics. You may decide they don't make the cut by the time you reach the end of the book, but that's up to you!

DATING EXAMPLES: Physical

You'll be happy you only used a maximum of two spaces for physical attributes because a man can be a perfect physical specimen and be zero of the other qualities that you're looking for, trust me. I'll give you an example.

The bodybuilder who loved himself more than any woman ever could

I was working out in a gym regularly because I wanted to see how fit I could get if I really applied myself. I was in the gym almost every day, sweating and feeling incredible. Apparently, I caught the eye of the gym's owner, a competitive bodybuilder whose impressive physique was plastered all over the gym in speedos and dark self-tanner.

He kept coming up to me, offering fitness advice, which was nice, but then he also kept asking me out. I thought he was good-looking, but I never really felt like there was any kind of attraction past that. He just read pretty one-dimensional to me. He also seemed a little cocky. It could be because he was in his gym, in his element, feeling powerful. All these things added up to me politely declining dates the first few times he asked.

Well, he persisted, and every time I'd go to the gym, he'd seek me out and we'd have a little chat generally based around fitness. Then he would ask me out on a date. One day I thought, "You know what, maybe I'm just writing him off too early. I've never been in a conversation with him outside of the gym. Maybe if I actually say yes to a date, I'll see another side to him." So the next time I went into the gym, I said yes, I'd go out to eat with him. He was excited, and we made plans for a few days from then. I told my sisters, who were jealous but told me that I was making a smart move. And they said that if I didn't want him, they'd be happy to take him off my hands.

Date night rolls around, and I'm fighting the feeling that it's not going to be spectacular. I thought to myself, "Now stop that. You said yes to this date because you want to give this guy a fair shot. So get dressed and be open to being surprised."

With that pep talk under my belt, I headed out the door with a smile, ready to be surprised by this guy. It couldn't be all bad. I mean, he's fit, handsome, and attentive so that's a really nice start, isn't it?

I get to dinner, and we exchange some banter, he's enthusiastic and trying to be entertaining, but we're not really able to get away from the topic of fitness and sex. I did like hearing about what the best things to be eating are. That was helpful for my fitness journey. I'm getting to listen to an expert's opinion, so that's valuable. I'm a big believer in taking my wins where I can!

What I couldn't shake were all the little gestures like trying to have a smoldering look on his face, which read more like allergies than bedroom eyes. Or he kept licking his lips slowly while looking at me, which was not sexy at all. It just felt creepy. Every time he exhibited one of these behaviors, I would ignore it and continue coming up with new topics of conversation. All of which he would reduce to something sexual. Ok, I see where this is going. I'm starting to feel like this date is precisely what I feared it would be. The bill comes, and I offer to split it, and he insists on covering it, which I thank him for. After he paid while checking out the waitress's backside in a not-subtle manner, we got up and headed outside. Charming.

We got outside, and he immediately tried to kiss me. I turn my head and put my hand on his chest to create some space between us.

Me: Hey! I already told you I don't kiss on a first date.

Him: What? Come on, baby, we had a nice night, right?

Me: I'm just not like that. I just wanted to go out and see if we had any chemistry.

He raises his eyebrows and smiles like he has won something.

Him: Yeah, so you're feeling it too, huh? Relax, it's not a big deal.

He tries to kiss me again. I push him off harder this time.

Me: Wait, what? No, that's not what I was getting at.

Him: Ah, come on, baby, you don't have to pretend you're not into it. I've seen how you look at me at the gym.

I'm officially upset now.

Me: How I look at you at the gym? Yes, you're very fit, but that's not why I said yes to this date.

He smiles a stomach-churning smile, clearly impressed with himself.

Him: Yeah...

Me: I was saying that I wanted to give you a fair shot since you kept asking me out. I thought that we'd probably not have much to talk about, and unfortunately, I was right.

Him: Did you really come out just to talk? I mean, come on...

He points and then waves his hands on either side of his body like a model showcasing a car on a game show. I shake my head and start to walk away. He jumps in front of me and makes a last-ditch effort to save the date.

Me: What are you doing? I'm leaving.

Him: You're really gonna say no to this? Come on, let's just go back to my place. You know you want to.

Me: Absolutely not. I'm not that kind of girl.

Him: Really? Do you know how many girls at the gym would kill to be in your place right now?

Me: Then ask one of them out. Honestly, I'd be more entertained with a poster of you on my wall than having another date with you.

He was in stunned silence as I walked to my car and drove off.

Key Takeaways from this interaction

1. I didn't trust my gut that we wouldn't have much in common. Gut instincts are often right, but sometimes, when your picker is broken, it's hard to know for sure.
2. He relied solely on his looks to get him, women. He spent no time developing a personality or manners. Being attracted to someone is important, but long-term relationships never succeed based on attributes that don't stand the test of time.
3. I am happy, however, that I went outside my comfort zone to test new types of men to date and add more information to my "Picker"!

This unfortunate soul thought that his physical fitness was the end all be all to his dating endeavors. Building an impressive body like his was an all-consuming focus for him and many other supremely fit men. I liked the health aspect of his world, but for him, it brought boatloads of entitlement and arrogance—two cardinal sins for me.

This is not to say that all fit men will be vapid self-obsessed jerks, but with him, there were signs.

He had zero interest in connecting at any more profound levels. This can be made very obvious in conversations as simple as "Why do you think fitness is important?" The answers vary wildly!

REFLECTION

Now the big question. What are your ideal guy's Physical Activity level, Diet, and Sleep regimen? Remember, this is one that you can take part in. This is a life you will share with him. So take a moment and think about what a wonderful day-to-day life looks like in these three categories.

Do you want a man who works out seven days a week and is in magazine-level shape? Are you ready to at least support him in that lifestyle, if not directly become a part of it? If you're not with him in the gym, are you happy to eat healthy food so it's not uncomfortable for him to share meals with you?

Perhaps it's actually more important that your partner will have a smile on their face while carrying all the picnic supplies and hiking to the top of your favorite waterfall to catch the sunset.

Or that they'll wake up early to catch the sunrise and stroll around the French Quarter of New Orleans while eating beignets and drinking chicory coffee?

Maybe they look great in cosplay and can handle a long day of the full comic-con experience, hitting every booth while stopping in between for posed pictures in character?

It could be as simple as they'll carry all the groceries in without whining about it. Then hang out in the kitchen cooking food you'll both enjoy.

This is personal. It's about you and what makes your heart happy!

The importance of having a similar lifestyle to your romantic interest is well-established in scientific literature. The old saying opposites attract does have merit in that different strengths can complement each other, but as far as your lifestyle goes, the more similar your daily activities are, the better.

"Among many monogamous species, from cockatiels to cichlid fish, studies have revealed a clear pattern: it helps to be more similar to your mate."
- Christian Jarrett BBC

How this goes on your list:

Now that you've taken a hard look at this physical dimension, what are your two purely physical traits? Only two traits, ladies, or you're heading in an unhelpful direction. Or maybe you want to use those spots for things like "Must be vegan," "Has kind eyes," or "Must be able to beat me in Twister"? There really are no rules! It's your list. Just make sure that each line you fill means something to you and your long-term happiness.

*Please don't completely disregard even one of these 8 Dimensions, though, as they will all work together to create a balanced and happy relationship, just as they work together to create a balanced and happy life.

Potential Physical Dimension "Must-Haves":

   1.

   2.

   3.

Brilliant Vixen Secret Bonus #1: Physical, aka Fun Ways to Meet Mr. Right using the Physical Dimension!

Changing your patterns of physical activity brings like-minded men into focus. If you decide that going to the gym more often is in alignment with your true self, then you'll be automatically surrounded by fitness-minded men the second you set foot in a gym. You're sharing an activity by virtue of location at that moment. There's no need to ask a man in the gym if he thinks fitness is important, that's one question that's already been answered for you, and the proof is in his actions.

This is the same if you like to go for walks in the park, do yoga, Martial arts, sports, dance classes, golf, or any other type of physical activity. Since diet is part of the physical dimension, let's not forget about cooking classes, Farmer's Markets, wine walks, and beer gardens. You're surrounded by an activity you enjoy, and you instantly have something in common with any man that's there. Believe me. The right man will notice that you share an interest in something they're also passionate about!

Want to cut the time meeting a guy in your activity in half? Please walk up to them and ask a question related to the activity. Now the door is wide open to learn more about each other.

Beginners' classes are incredible because you're both at the same spot in your journey into your activity, where you've taken the first giant step in showing up and putting your time into an interest.

Now that we've taken the first step let's go even further into how our Mr. Right is going to be spending a great deal of his time. The following section deals with a potential deal-breaker that could have you asking for the bill after the first drinks arrive.

Chapter Two

OCCUPATIONAL

A job is how you make money. A career is how you make your mark. A calling is how you acknowledge a higher vision, whatever it may be" -Deepak Chopra.

Ah, yes, this is where I write down exactly what kind of doctor or celebrity he is, right?

I'm afraid not, my dear. In this dimension of wellness, we're looking at how he's chosen to make a living. Not in terms of money per se, but even more revealing than that. We need to find out exactly what his world at work entails. Even more revealing yet is measuring the personal satisfaction your potential mate receives from what he's dedicated his life to. All of it comes into play for the long term and your future happiness.

The path that a man takes with his career tells you loads about what's important to him. This is where he chooses to put the majority of his time and energy. If he's chosen wisely, he finds his work enriching and truly rewarding. Yes, the monetary value of his work is important, but we'll discuss that in the next chapter, as it's an entirely different subject.

A man who loves what he does for a living has a beautiful vibrancy to him. That's something you want to be near because that kind of joy is hard to beat.

Think of his work as his favorite activity times 10. He's choosing to spend a large portion of his life here, so this is extremely telling.

> *"If we take the average amount of hours worked per week, which was 39.2 hours in 2014 according to the annual survey of hours and earnings, then you will work a total of 92,120 hours in the course of your working life (based on a rough calculation of 39.2 hours *(52-5 = 47 weeks to take account of holidays)*50 years)." - Karl Thompson, revisesociology.com.*

So he's going to spend over ninety-two thousand hours doing this activity. Make sure it's one you find acceptable. If you find an issue with his chosen career and hope he will choose differently someday, then you are setting yourself up for disappointment. If you find his line of work objectionable, then that's an immediate game-over situation.

There's no need to pursue anything further. Whatever you do, ladies, for your own happiness, do not, I repeat, do not look at him as a project. This is fertile ground for resentment for both parties, and it's a ghastly place to put your energy. Supporting a man while he shoots for the stars is loving and wonderful. Seeing a man as a fixer-upper is doomed from the get-go.

His career choice can also be a giant canary in a gold-mine situation. If he's miserable in his chosen profession, why is he choosing such a joyless life? What underlying mechanisms are pushing him in that direction? What will that look like when he spends time with you at the end of his work day? A man who doesn't enjoy what he does for a living is already at a happiness deficit, and that is not someone to build a life with. So for your own happiness, just assume that his career choice is here to stay. There, now that's sorted. I had to mention that because I've heard ladies on dates testing the waters for possible career changes or asking about promotions and how they could get them. Needless to say, the results were not rewarding.

As with all things on the list, let's take a deeper look at what it looks like to be around his chosen profession.

What are the hours like?

Is this a night job, and do you work during the day? How would you spend any time together? Is he on-call? Liam used to have an on-call job many years ago, and he quit because it made him feel unstable and completely unable to ever fully relax. I didn't come along and convince him to leave. That job was long gone before we ever met. His decisions were very telling to me about what he valued, and happiness ranked very high on his list, just like mine.

What are the conditions?

For example, is it a dangerous line of work? If so, will you be able to handle the daily uncertainty? There are no guarantees in life, and definitely not one that nothing bad will ever happen, but if his line of work has a core element of danger, how will you process that? Liam is friends with a retired police officer, and he told me that this man and his wife would eat breakfast every day, he would put on his uniform, and they would hold each other with great intention before he left for work every day. He would call her in his downtime and try to assure her that he was as safe as he could be. That worked for them but would it work for you?

Who is he surrounded by all day?

Like the example of the professional fighter, who is he surrounded by all day long? Does that idea make you feel uncomfortable? For instance, if he ran a modeling agency, would it make you feel uncomfortable that he's surrounded by beautiful women all day or would it not bother you at all? This quickly turns to my next point...

What are the cultural values of that profession?

Is he in a profession where caring for others is part of the job? Do his reasons for being in that job reflect that as a priority in life? Some women mistakenly put a specific career on their list because they assume that it means that a man will possess certain traits or qualities. I have found that it can lead to fewer choices while dating and also disappointment that some men have chosen that occupation for surprisingly different reasons than they had hoped.

Is he surrounded by fast-talking stock brokers who value money above all else? Then the common workplace culture revolves around status, and you'll be expected to reflect that from how you look and dress to where you go on vacation.

Does he spend his time with gruff men who make off-color comments? That salty language and some of those opinions will make their way into your relationship. Those values will have a direct influence on him and guide his life in both subtle and not-so-subtle ways.

The shared values of his profession can definitely come into play as most people don't have a clear delineation between work life and private life. If you're spending half your life at work, then you've chosen to immerse yourself in that workplace culture.

Dating Example: Occupational

Wait...you do what for a living?

This next story is from a friend of mine, let's call her "Amy." Well, my lovely friend "Amy" had gone on a few dates with a man she met through a dating site. Amy said she'd had fun with him and that he was handsome and attentive to her, but she didn't know if she could date him anymore.

I was puzzled. So I started firing off some questions. Eventually, we got to the source of the problem. His occupation.

Me: "So what does he do for a living?"

Amy: "Yeah, that's the problem... he's a stripper."

Me: "Oh, I see."

Amy: "I'm just not really able to see how I'm going to be serious about him if he's dancing like that for other girls."

Me: "That's definitely a boundary that would be difficult to navigate."

Amy: "But he's so cute!"

Me: "Well darling, he probably wouldn't make any money if he wasn't. That's not the issue at hand. Whom he's surrounded by and what he's doing while he's at work is clearly bothering you."

Amy: "He's already said that he has no other skills that would give him the same income, and he obviously has no immediate plans to change careers."

Me: "What do you think is left to be done?"

Amy: "I guess I'm just going to have to let this one go. It's always harder with the cute ones, isn't it!"

Key Takeaways from this interaction

Even though Amy really liked everything else about this man, what he did for a living was difficult for her. He was in great shape, handsome, attentive to her needs, and spoiled her with gifts because he had plenty of money. The problem was that it was all in one-dollar bills. I already told Amy I was going to put that in the book, and we had a good laugh about it!

1. Whom he was surrounded by at work made Amy uncomfortable.

2. The very nature of his work made Amy uncomfortable

This type of situation was not something that was going to improve with time or any other factor. He checked all the rest of Amy's boxes but in a manner that made her uncomfortable every time she thought about it.

His occupational dimension would have ended the relationship eventually. It's just a matter of how long Amy wanted to delude herself and honestly lead herself and this man along.

REFLECTION

Here's another extreme example of how a man's workplace culture can affect you. Are you dating someone in public office? Then you really have to adhere to a set of rules so as not to hurt his chances for re-appointment. Those cultural values might include not being controversial in any way or publicly demonstrating a very particular set of values. Are you comfortable with that?

What about a college professor? Chances are that workplace culture will center around intellectual pursuits. Is discussing classic works of literature and schools of philosophical thought your happy place? Do you value your own ongoing educational pursuits? Would you enjoy accompanying him to conventions and lectures on topics that coincide with his field of expertise?

These are just a few examples to get you thinking about what the cultural values of any given occupation are. Some are obvious, and you'll know what's involved from the moment the profession is mentioned. Some seem obvious but will surprise you! Others might take a little time to figure out. In any case, it's essential to consider this when selecting a romantic partner.

This is not to say that if you're dating a mechanic whose work garage has centerfolds posted on the walls that he's automatically a misogynist. As a matter of fact, my mechanic is a family run business where everyone is respectful, caring and they take great pride in their work. Plenty of men have jobs like plumber, welder and construction manager simply because they enjoy fixing or building things. It can be really satisfying to create something as important as a home with your own two hands! Many of these jobs are not only more emotionally rewarding than most women understand but they can also be more financially rewarding than you would think. It's worth it to take a moment and find out why someone has chosen their career as it's often more important in the long run than where they're currently working.

As the quote at the beginning of this chapter points out, this dimension will definitely show if this man is living his passion and has a calling or not. It also may show you what kind of a mark he would like to leave on the world. Being with someone who's passionate about what they do for a living will create an incredible light in your life. It's an underrated dimension that most people look at in a way that doesn't tell the whole story.

When you ask a man what he does for a living, you're looking for passion and compatibility. Plain and simple. That passion for his career shows that he will go after something that he loves and cherish it. That shows a mindset for consistent happiness, which is incredible. Anyone can chase money which we'll address next.

Here are the two questions to ask yourself when talking to a guy.

Is he passionate about what he does?

Is this a good fit for you?

That's it. Just two questions to consider at the end of the day. You have all the background context you need from this chapter, so when it's game time, you just think about these two points.

How this goes on your list:

As you may already be able to tell, I am a big fan of these points, being less about a specific career and more about a lifestyle. My list just had "Passionate about his work" on it. There were definitely occupations that would have been deal breakers but no one single occupation that was a necessity. You may put something like "Flexible vacation time" if the freedom of spontaneous trips is deeply important to you. Possibly "Makes enough for me to stay at home with the kids" if marriage and kids are the most important aspect of a relationship for you. I do caution against rushing too quickly in that direction, though. "Hi, do you want to take 100% of the responsibility for supporting me and our unborn children?" is hardly first-date talk!

You may decide there isn't anything specific that has

to do with "Occupation" that really needs to be on your list of "Must-Haves" or "Deal-Breakers." That's also alright! Or you may figure out that the reason you had "Firefighter" on your list is actually because "Brave" or "Cares for his community" is truly the thing that matters to you, and you had mistakenly only associated it with a specific career.

So here are three spots max that is associated with career.

1.

2.

3.

Brilliant Vixen Secret Bonus #2: Occupational aka Fun Ways to Meet Mr. Right using the Occupational Dimension!

So when you've stopped to think about what types of work cultures you really enjoy, be sure to factor that in when planning how to use your free time. For example, if you really like adventure-related work cultures, then sign up for a wilderness first aid course. You're bound to meet backpacking guides, search and rescue teams etc. They're there for professional training, and you'll get an inside look at how they spend their free time. If you enjoy the culture, you're bound to meet men in that profession. Perhaps you'd be happier at a Mensa lecture, where you're more likely to meet someone in an academic field. Sometimes it's not a perfectly straight line. Think about all the different kinds of professionals who enjoy golf or wine tasting. Besides, who doesn't love taking a fun class or just learning something new?

As always, I would never recommend you do something in order to "catch" a man and definitely never, ever do anything that would "trick" a man. Think about how that would make you feel if the shoe was on the other foot. Rather do things you actually enjoy! Putting genuine effort into meeting the right person should be gratifying for you and flattering for the person you end up spending time with.

Men who are investing their time into occupational pursuits are also investing their money into those pursuits. This brings us to our third dimension of wellness.

Chapter Three

FINANCIAL

It's good to have money and the things that money can buy, but it's good, too, to check up once in a while and make sure that you haven't lost the things that money can't buy. -George Lorimer

Money is important. There's no debating that. When it comes to the idea of money and romance, that focus changes.

Discussing finances on the surface might not be the most romantic topic, but it is important. Dating is about making sure that you're setting yourself up for a great life with someone you're romantically interested in. Part of that is determining if you're financially compatible.

Everyone is different. We each have different tolerances for financial stability. Some prefer to create as large a safety net as possible while planning for their future, and that's valid. Others of us like to throw caution to the wind when it comes to finances as long as all the other boxes are checked. That is also valid.

I myself am more in the second category. I looked at the entirety of my relationship with Liam and said, "Let the chips fall where they may. He's perfect for me in every other way," and I never looked back. He had just left working with fighters as a full-time living and was 100% invested in a fresh start. I had no idea what that would look like, and I didn't care.

It turned out great, and we've had much better adventures since he switched career paths. He is vibrant and happy now, and we're doing great, by the way. The one thing that made me feel secure was that I believed in his passion for finding the next thing that would generate money for him. He's a passionate guy who's brilliant, so I knew he'd hit his stride given time, and I wouldn't have to carry the financial responsibilities alone. He did, but to the outside world, it was a risk.

What made this dimension still work for me with Liam was that we agreed on finances in general. We decided what was essential to spend money on. For us, that's making sure that we never feel limited as we explore the world and anything that keeps a feeling of magic alive. Sometimes our budgets were limited, but we had the biggest experiences we could within those budgets!

There are a million things we could each decide to spend money on, and when we talked about what we like to do with our money, the answers that came up were very similar. It was never about the specifics of income. It was more about the financial priorities that we had in common. Most people wouldn't list "magic" or "adventure" as financial priorities right next to "food" and "shelter." We both did!

Those conversations we had together on dates really solidified how we viewed the world together and now how we raise our daughter together. Income fluctuates over a lifetime but priorities, although they evolve, are generally more consistent as they stem from core values.

Ladies, whatever you do, please don't ever just blurt out, "So, how much money do you make?" Most quality men will immediately see the question as off-putting and lower their opinion of you. It inevitably reads as "gold digger" in bright neon letters.

I've actually seen this happen in person when I was having a night out. I saw an attractive couple having drinks and enjoying a lovely night out, all smiles and loveliness...right up to the point where the girl smiled and said, "So, like, how much do you make?" The man immediately stopped laughing, and a puzzled look crept over his face. "What?" he said, visibly taken aback by the faux pa. She tilted her head in a cutesy way and said "Stop, I don't mean it like that. I just mean, are you still working your way up at your company, or are you good?" Seeing the disappoint-ment on his face was devastating. I looked away and never saw the end of that date.

The point is there's no amount of playful banter that can undo that fun-shattering question. It immediately puts the entire focus of the date on the man's earning power and not on the rest of who they are.

If you opt instead for questions about what they like to do for fun and what their special treats are for themselves when they accomplish significant milestones, that will give you a much more well rounded view of who they are when it comes to finances. The subject of finances while dating shouldn't be about exactly how much either of you are making but rather about how you choose to spend the money you have. If one person enjoys extensive traveling and the other enjoys staying home and collecting cars you can see how this would be a problem no matter how the income is scaled up or down. Or if one person enjoys saving as much as possible in order to enjoy an early retirement and the other would prefer to enjoy the journey with shopping sprees and vacations along the way. These differing ideologies are quite likely to cause disagreements, and financial disagreements are the number one indicator of divorce.

"These findings suggest that financial disagreements are stronger predictors of divorce relative to other common marital disagreements." https://onlineli-brary.wiley.com

---

I believe that the reason financial disagreements are the number one indicator of divorce is not because money is the most important thing. In fact, many financial disagreements happen not because a couple is in financial distress but because they disagree on how to spend the money they have. How you choose to spend your money speaks very clearly about what your priorities are in life.

Liam and I both value our relationship, family and the memories we make together above all else. Here are a few examples of what that currently looks like for us. We both work, so we both save money year-round in order to make the holidays special for our loved ones and each other. We show love with consistent quality time together at home and save for trips as often as we can. We generally don't spend much money on dinners out and choose to save by making meals at home. Sometimes I do most of the cooking, and sometimes it's Liam....ok. He might see this! I admit it; mostly, it's Liam. But I almost always make sure his laundry is clean and pressed, so we rarely need to take anything to the cleaners!

We are a partnership, and in all things, we try to contribute in a balanced way. Now that doesn't mean that we can always both contribute to financial goals evenly. Sometimes my income has been higher, and sometimes Liam's has been. We also can't always contribute to the household in a balanced way as sometimes one of us is on a crazy deadline (like right now, publishing this book!), but we both find ways to contribute, and I think that's incredibly important.

Sometimes financial contribution isn't something you're willing/able to do. Are you a more traditional woman who would enjoy being a homemaker? If so, then this might be a path worth pursuing. Before anyone writes me a letter about the patriarchy, I am a feminist who supports women in their choices. There's nothing wrong with a woman(or a man!) choosing to be a homemaker. In fact, it takes a great deal of courage in this day and age to choose this path. No one path is correct for all women, so please do not judge your sisters so harshly for noble choices like caring for children full-time. Now that I've voiced my support for all women, back to my point.

This time spent working in the household is a significant contribution for the woman(or man) who has chosen to be a full-time homemaker. Just how common is this scenario in modern times? The answer might surprise you.

"According to the Pew Research Center, roughly one in five U.S. adults are stay-at-home parents."
"According to 2019 data from Salary.com, if you are a stay-at-home parent and paid for your services, you would be looking at a median annual salary of $178,201."-Salary.com. *'How Much Is a Mother Really Worth?' Why? Because many stay-at-home parents work around the clock. If you have young children, work can often mean nighttime feed-*

ings, greeting early morning risers, and late-night meal prep." -Porcshe Moran, Investopedia https://www.investopedia.com/financial-edge/0112/how-much-is-a-homemaker-worth.aspx

Let's take a moment to appreciate that. $178,201 is what all the services provided by a stay-at-home parent would be worth! $66,755 is the average salary in the US for 2022. Please also keep in mind that this was calculated based on childcare, late-night feedings, early-morning meal prep, cleaning, laundry services etc. All of these things and more were done to contribute to the household.

What ultimately makes for a great couple is that you're a team in every way. This can take more forms than I can possibly list but here are a few more examples....

The wife of a fighter who preps every meal for him, weighing and separately packaging them for precise nutritional and calorie count. She also washes every sweaty sock and drives him back and forth to the gym during fight camp because he's too exhausted to be safe on the roads.

The musician's wife who photographs every gig and

then stays up till the wee hours of the morning wrapping cords and packing gear out.

The author's wife who proofreads all his work and discusses it in detail with him before he sends it off to his editor.

The construction worker's wife, who drives lunch over to his job site so he can have a hot meal and a cold drink in the middle of a hard day.

Partners of all kinds who look for the little things which make their significant other's life just a little bit easier or more enjoyable.

You need to be able to lean on each other and take on the world together! We're looking for our soulmate when we're dating and having fun along the way.

Healthy relationships rely on a balance between the two people in them. Expecting one person to do absolutely everything in a relationship is not a caring mindset, and it will not yield long-lasting happiness.

Love is about wanting to take care of each other. When you're looking at the entirety of a relationship, your natural inclination should be to take care of the other person in the relationship. If you're choosing the right person, they should be just as interested in taking care of you as you are in taking care of them.

So to recap, money is important. There's no denying that. One of the most common causes of stress and, unfortunately, divorce is financial disagreements. Arguing about money early on is a big red flag, and the underlying reasons for that argument should be given careful consideration when deciding whether to continue the relationship.

"Nearly half of Americans (48%) who are married or living with a partner say they argue with the person over money, according to a survey of more than 1,000 people by The Cashlorette, which is owned by personal finance site Bankrate.com. Most of those fights are about spending habits, with 60% saying that one person spends too much or the other is too cheap. The remaining fights are pretty evenly split between someone being dishonest about money, how to divide the bills and other types of money fights, which could be anything from disagreements over forgetting to pay a bill to a couple's financial priorities in life." - Catey Hill MarketWatch.

"At least two studies show that this could lead to divorce. Data released Wednesday by financial firm TD Ameritrade found that 41% of divorced Gen Xers and 29% of Boomers say they ended their marriage due to disagreements about money. What's more, if you're arguing about

money early on in your relationship, watch out: That may be the No. 1 predictor of whether or not you'll end up divorced, according to a study of more than 4,500 couples published in the journal Family Relationships." - Catey Hill MarketWatch.

I have a couple of examples of dates that went poorly, just based on the financial dimension. The exciting thing is that in neither of the examples were the men financially lacking, at least not from my point of view. It's how their personal relationships with money were handled that made things go south. It affected every aspect of their personalities and made the mismatch glaringly obvious to anyone who knew how to look for it.

Dating Examples: Financial

Well, that was undoubtedly efficient.

I went on a coffee date with a man who was an efficiency expert for Fortune 500 corporations. He asked me out for a day date, and I thought, why not? I could use a coffee and some conversation. He was attractive and energetic, and I thought it sounded like fun.

We met at a small vibey coffee shop and sat down by

a big picture window overlooking the parking lot. He immediately told me what he did for a living, and my response was, "Oh, cool! Like Lucy Liu's character, where she dressed like a dominatrix to distract everyone while her partners spied on the company?" I expected a laugh or at least a little chuckle. Nothing, crickets. He just wrinkled his eyebrows a little bit and said, "What?" I replied, "Nothing, just a silly movie reference." I was a little surprised that he didn't even ask me which movie, just carried on talking about his job responsibilities. Even though he was speaking so quickly that I had to have an internal chuckle about how efficient this efficiency expert was being, I actually found it quite interesting. Which was good because it was so hard to get more than a word or two in edgewise that I mostly just smiled and nodded. I had been a manager before at some stunningly inefficient companies and we did have a little laugh over that. Everything was going reasonably well, but there was just one odd thing that kept popping up.

He kept bringing the conversation back around to his car. He was smart, quick-witted, and he had a great smile, but no matter what we were discussing, he kept trying to steer the conversation back to his car as he made vague gestures towards the parking lot outside of the window.

I'm not really a car person so I didn't really look too hard to see what he was gesturing towards. He kept persisting until he finally just pointed at a yellow car in the parking lot and blurted out, "That's my Ferrari! Have you ever been in one?" I smiled and giggled a little bit. The urgency with which he said it just hit me in a funny way. I said, "I don't think so. I'm not much of a car person although there are some classic cars that I think are really gorgeous." He looked so deflated that I felt bad for him. I tried to recover to make him feel better "But they're really nice, right? I bet it's fun to drive."

After several more failed topics of conversation the date ended, we walked outside, and he showed me his car. In his defense, it was a stunning yellow Ferrari. I said, "Oh, that is a beautiful car, isn't it?" He saw that I liked it and got excited.

Him: "Maybe for our next date, I can pick you up, and we can go for a drive."
Me: "Oh, cool," I said, trying to be polite.
He smiled and said...
Him: "You know what? I had such a good time on this date...I have to go to France for work. How about I pick you up in this car, and we fly off together for your second date?"
Me: "That's a very generous offer, but I like to get to

know someone a little better before I travel with them internationally. But thank you again. That's so generous of you."

I gracefully thanked him for a lovely time and called it a day. There was no second date. He was so fixated on his fancy car and his abundant finances that it was like the only things he had to offer were all money-related. He hadn't asked me any questions about my life or offered much about his own that wasn't financially centered. That caused me great concern that he didn't have anything else to talk about. Even when I asked him about the interesting places he had been to, the answers were all about how he'd flown there first class and eaten at really expensive restaurants. He never shared what kind of food, just that it was expensive.

Personally, I have been to amazing hole-in-the-wall restaurants as well as restaurants with a coveted Michelin 3-star rating. For me, it's never about how expensive the restaurant is. It's about how enjoyable the food and ambiance are. Similarly, travel is all about the richness of the experiences and the memories I made along the way. As well as the people I met and the connections I made. None of these types of details were important enough for this man to include in his stories as they clearly

didn't hold the same value for him as they do
for me.

The fact that his whole self-worth was tied up in
wealth spoke volumes about what he thought he had
to offer to women. I was very upfront with him when
we chatted next and told him that I felt that he was
leading with his money and that what I was looking
for was a deeper connection. This was a moment
where he still could have chosen to pivot the conversation but didn't. As the conversation ended, I told
him to be wary of what he's leading with because
there's a risk that the kind of girl who would be
drawn in with just material possessions might say yes
to future dates for less than genuine reasons.

A man with resources is a really nice bonus, but if he's
not the one for you, then you're not going to find a
joyful life together in a line at the bank teller. I grew
up poor, so I understand that from the outside, it
looks like expensive trips and cars make you happy. I
can tell you from personal experience, though, that it
is possible to be someplace beautiful and have it
utterly ruined by whoever you're there with. It is also
possible to be someplace mundane and have it be
amazing because of the company you're with.

Of course, what we're aiming for with all you Brilliant

Vixen's is for you to be someplace spectacular with someone who lights you up even in a dark room!

Key Takeaways from this interaction

1. His self-worth was so deeply ingrained in his wealth that without me reacting to it in the way he wanted, he ran out of topics of conversation. Can you imagine what that looks like long term? And what does that look like for him or you if he loses his fortune?

2. He didn't know what else to offer me as a partner other than his wealth. This spoke to me of an inability to form real connections. So I didn't really get to know him that well, and I suspect that time would not have changed that.

3. The details he chose to share in his stories highlighted what he valued and prioritized. I could then evaluate whether these values and priorities lined up with my own. They did not.

The Hunger Games

I met this guy on a dating app like more and more people do every day in modern times, and we agreed to meet at a bar/grill lounge. After several conversations on the app, he seemed normal enough, so I didn't have a ton of reservations about the meet-up. The day of the date came around, and I told him that I was delighted that he had suggested meeting up for food and drinks at a restaurant. I was STARVING after a long day at work! I made that point abundantly clear before I even showed up; this is important.

I was listening to my stomach growling the whole drive over, and I pulled up to the restaurant, relieved to finally get to eat. We greeted each other, and I immediately started looking for the menu while holding my stomach with one hand. We were chatting, and the waitress came and took our drink orders. A drink sounded brilliant to unwind while I looked at the menu, and then I could focus on the date properly.

Our drinks came rather quickly, and the waitress said she'd be right back to take our order and exited promptly. I was laughably sad to see her go, but I thought ok, one last glance at the menu. I'm still being pleasant and keeping up some lively banter while waiting for the waitress to return. I catch her eye, and she smiles and comes running back. To my absolute horror, my date looks at her in disgust and angrily waves her away. She raises an eyebrow and mouths "wow" to herself as she quickly turns away and leaves. I was traumatized, so hungry, and I looked at my date in bewilderment. He just kept talking about his job and didn't have the slightest reaction to my agape jaw. I took a sip from my drink and looked at the menu again. The waitress saw me glancing around for her and walked over to check on us. "Did you guys decide on something?" she said sweetly and incredibly patiently, especially considering my date's rudeness. He looked at her again like she was an idiot and said, "No, we're fine," with so much arrogance and overwhelming disdain that I was instantly repulsed. I had officially had it with this behavior, and I got up and walked after the waitress. "I'm sorry, I have no idea what that's about. Could I please order the crab cakes, and could you please put that on my bill?" she smiled and said, "Absolutely, sweetie, I'll get that right out." Relief does not begin to cover how I felt at that moment.

I returned to the table, and he asked, "What was that about?" I said, "I'm starving, so I ordered an appetizer. I've been working all day and mentioned that I couldn't wait to eat on the phone. Don't worry. I put it on my tab." He shrugged and raised both his eyebrows dismissively. "Ok," he replied, seeming annoyed for some inconceivable reason. My appetizer arrives, and it's three crab cakes, just three teeny tiny crab cakes. I looked up at my heroine of appetizers and thanked her, "Thank you so much. I'm starving." I excitedly grabbed the first crab cake and blissfully started munching away. At that moment, I didn't even care that there were only three of them on the plate. I knew it would be just barely enough for me not to feel faint.

Mr. Wrong was busy talking about how right now, he's an apprentice associate making $40k a year, but he's next in line to be a Junior Associate in a year, so he'll be making a cool $65k after that. Oh, and don't forget that in 5 years, he'll be making $80K, "So you know things are looking up for me," he said with a punchable smirk on his face. I'd already decided that his chances of a second date were already teetering on the brink of non-existent. But perhaps he was acting like an obnoxious preppie throwback in an effort to impress me. It was not going well.

Then, he commits the most egregious sin my blood-sugar levels could handle under the circumstances. He looks at my plate, grabs one of my crab cakes and stuffs it in his mouth and keeps talking with his mouth full. I was horrified that he was eating what little food I had left. I look at him like he's on fire, and he says, "Ugh, too salty," as he reaches for the menu and looks at the price. "And they're way over-priced too. Figures." What? Why? I'm so hungry, and not only do you take my food, but you insult it as you cram it in your pretentious little mouth.

That's it. I'm gone. Sorted. I waved the waitress over and asked for the checks. He looks surprised that I'm ready to leave. He walked me to my car, continuing to drone on about something irrelevant. I think it was that he was going to buy a Mercedes tomorrow or something. Who knows. What's important is that I went and got a foot-long sandwich and a chocolate chip cookie and went home to eat in peace. There we are. That's the kind of food satisfaction I needed. I spent the remainder of the evening feeling well-fed and satisfied, which was a lovely change of pace.

The next day he rang me up and asked me out on another date. I couldn't believe he thought the first date went well, so I knew he needed to have it spelled out for him.

Him: "Hey, I had fun yesterday. Too bad you had to go. I just thought I'd hit you up and invite you out again. You busy Friday?"
Me: "No, thank you. I would not like to go out on a second date with you."
Him: "Really, why not? I thought we had a great time?"
Me: "I did not, actually. I told you very clearly on the

way there that I was starving and that I had just gotten off work, so I wouldn't have a chance to eat before our date."

Him: "Oh...well, I thought you were just trying to get a free meal out of me."

Me: "Excuse me? For starters, I paid for my own food."

Him: "Well, I didn't know you were gonna do that."

Me: "You invited me out for food and drinks. You knew I was hungry, you were super rude to the waitress, and you didn't care that I was uncomfortable. You just kept talking about how much money you were making. Don't ask a lady out for "food and drinks" and then not only ignore her discomfort but also actively prevent her from getting food. That doesn't make me feel like you care if I'm uncomfortable or not."

Him: "Oh...well, I've had girls just want free meals out of me before. So I just decided I'm not going to pay for women's food anymore."

I take a deep breath.

Me: "A few things here. Let's start with this, how do you know these women just used you for food?"

Him: "Well, they didn't want second dates."

Me: "If they just wanted a free meal, then why wouldn't they have wanted a second free meal? Could it actually be that they didn't enjoy themselves on the first date?"

Him: "Oh..."

Me: "That brings me to my second point. All you wanted to talk about is how much money you were making and how much money you were going to make in the future."

Him: "Yeah, well, women care about that stuff, so you have to let them know, or they won't want to date you."

Me: "Not all women. I don't care as much about that as knowing that a guy will want me to be happy and feel cared for. That's not a money thing. That's a nurturing thing."

Him: "Oh. I'm sorry. Hey, how about I take you to dinner tonight? You can order whatever you want, on me."

Me: "Apology accepted. I'll have to decline the invitation. Please make sure the next girl you take on a date is comfortable, ok?"

Him: "Oh, ok. See you."

Key Takeaways from this interaction

1. He was so fixated on not being taken advantage of financially that he disregarded my comfort to protect either his pocketbook or his pride. Anyone who would let you go hungry isn't the type of person that you want on your team as you navigate life's ups and downs.

2. His poor treatment of the waitress could have been indicative of disdain for anyone perceived to be making less money than him. It could also show how he treats anyone he's not trying to impress. Either way it does not say good things about how he treats others.

3. His earning power was clearly where all of his self-worth came from, as that was the only thing he wanted to talk about on the date. This behavior shows a lack of balance in life.

A little side note on the paying for dinner issue.

How do you feel about a man paying for dinner?

You don't have to offer to pay for anything on the first date if he's the one who invited you out, but it would go a long way toward making a man feel deeply appreciated if you offer to pay for a little something on the second date. It can be as small as offering to take him out for ice cream or coffee and letting him know it's your treat. It sounds funny, but that small act would set you apart from most women that he goes out on a date with. This shows that you're serious about being a long-term partner.

Personally, as a feminist, I think it's very acceptable

to split the dinner bill on the first date. Another way that it could be done is that if he picks up the bill, you can offer to pay for the next one or offer to get the tip. If you get up and leave the restaurant, you can offer to buy some drinks at the following location or date.

At the end of the day, it's up to you how you feel about who pays on a first date. If you're more traditional and believe a man should pay for all the dates, that's your prerogative. I like to have a feeling of balance in as many areas of life as I can, so I want dates to feel balanced, also. In making your list, I wouldn't recommend making this a black or white subject line as far as he needs to do one or the other, but instead, I would suggest writing down how you want to feel on the date.

For example:
Respected
Seen
Safe
Cared for

I recommend this approach because maybe you split the bill, but you felt like he respected you, was attentive and still made you feel cared for because he gave you his jacket when he saw you were cold. In another scenario you don't discuss it at all, and he asks to have the bill split and seems combative about it. That would be a red flag for me because it indicates a possible disdain for women. Or maybe he paid the entire bill and then pressured you for something physical, so you felt disrespected and unsafe. How a man makes you feel on a first date is him on his best behavior, so if that feels off to you, then there's very little chance of a happy and healthy relationship.

Another side note on the concept of "I'm an Independent Woman!":

Being an independent woman is identical to being a functional adult. A woman who pays for her own things and takes care of herself is checking all the boxes that society expects adults to handle. If you're doing this, then my hats off to you, it's not easy. But please don't fall into the "I don't need a man, I pay my own bills" confrontational mindset. Yes, clearly, you're able to pay for your own things because you showed up for the date without assistance, looking fabulous. This requires a substantial amount of effort, planning, and resources. He already assumes that you pay for all your own stuff, as he didn't front any of the money involved for you to show up to the date, so there's no conflict there. Only a particular music group made this non-issue seem like a point of contention, in my opinion. So relax, ladies. He knows you've got this!

By default, he assumes you're an independent woman. Now he's looking for a partner just as you are. If he's not, then he'll stick out like a sore thumb once you start asking him real questions that relate to your new list.

Reflection:

What are your life goals, and how do they relate to financial goals?
i.e., Children, world travel, early retirement or adventure etc.

Are you a spender or a saver?

What's worth splurging on in life?

How do you see yourself contributing to the financial well-being of a relationship?

These are some fundamental questions to ask yourself as you craft your future. What kind of life is a fulfilling life for you? Get it down on paper and work backward from that. In all fairness, if you can pay for approximately half of it, then it's highly attainable with a partner in life. If you have not previously been thinking of this dimension in terms of a true partnership, then some reflection will certainly highlight that and encourage growth in this area. There are ebbs and flows to who can contribute what in any relationship, and that's what being a real couple is all about. We're building long-lasting love and intimacy in every department, even the bills.

How this goes on your list:

Take a look back at your "Reflection" notes. See if there are any qualities or priorities that you tend to repeat in different ways.
i.e., Adventurous/Adventure, Frugal/Safe, Children/family oriented

These are great clues to what is truly important enough to make it on your list!

Potential Financial Dimension "Must-Haves":
1.

2.

3.

Brilliant Vixen Secret Bonus #3: Financial

aka Fun Ways to Meet Mr. Right using the Financial Dimension!

Searching out activities which are complementary to the lifestyle you enjoy is a great way to meet people that you would enjoy spending time with.

As an example let's say you like to dress up in vintage 50's clothing and visit old-fashioned cute places like antiques stores and little diners with malt shops. Yes, please! I'll totally go with you. I have the perfect hats and dresses! Oops I got a little carried away, back to my point. You put on an adorable vintage outfit, and instead of going to a vintage store, you head over to a rockabilly convention with a car show. The men there are wholly dedicated to that lifestyle, and they put their money where their mouth is. They might even have a vintage car in the car show portion. Here in Las Vegas, there's always a car show attached to these events.

The point I'm trying to make is that they're investing in the same area you are. It's just in a slightly different yet highly complimentary way. You're never going to have to ask them if they want to go to this type of convention because they're already polishing up their chrome bumper for the next one without you saying a word. That's a lot of compatibility without a word being spoken about if it's meaningful to him or not.

This is about seeing where he wants to spend his money and showing you what's important to him. Since we're talking about where he spends his money, this naturally leads us straight to the next point, where does he spend his time?

Chapter Four

ENVIRONMENTAL

"You are a product of your environment. So choose the environment that will best develop you toward your objective. Analyze your life in terms of its environment. Are the things around you helping you toward success - or are they holding you back?"

- W. Clement Stone

This dimension speaks to the physical spaces that you inhabit. This includes your home, workspace and the space where you spend the majority of your free time.

Are your spaces ones that stimulate and provide a feeling of well-being? Did you know that:

" Research shows our physical environments significantly influence our cognition, emotions and subsequent behaviors, including our relationships with others?" -Sander, Elizabeth (Libby) J., et al. "Psychological Perceptions Matter: Developing the Reactions to the Physical Work Environment Scale."

So as we look at building a life with someone, it's only natural to take a look at the spaces we will spend that life in.

Home space:

The first one we'll look at is our Home space. Our homes are our most private refuge from the rest of the world. This is where we go to recharge and replenish. If you're having a tough day, going home should be the most comforting idea you can think of. What choices have you made regarding your home? Even within the same city, like here in Las Vegas, there are vastly different options, from high-rise condominiums to homes nestled in the mountains surrounding the valley. There are apartments out in the suburbs and ones in the center of downtown. If you live in a small town, there might be different options, like a log cabin down a long dirt road versus right in the middle of town where the roads are always plowed in the winter.

What have you chosen to do with the interior of your home? Is it modern and minimal, eclectic and maximalist or something in between? Have you put care and thought into it, or are there still partially unpacked boxes from your last move? If it isn't currently your ideal living situation, then have you thought about what that would look like? Do you have strong feelings about your space, or are you more flexibly minded about possible options?

A recent study on ScienceDirect.com has shown that a cluttered space is detrimental to psychological well-being, but what if your idea of being cluttered and your partners differ wildly? For some, a maximalist aesthetic is warm and feels cozy, like you're surrounded by all the things you love, but for others, it would feel like overwhelming chaos. In contrast, Minimalism feels clean, organized and calming for some, but it feels sterile, cold and depressing for others. Do you know where you fall on this spectrum?

Have you visited or lived in spaces that created anxiety and depression versus ones that nurtured feelings of calm and joy? Can you imagine living every day in either of those extremes? This is why we're going to take a look at what your ideal living situation is so that when you are dating, you can take a look at your potential partner's living situation and see if it's a match or at least close enough that both people could find a way to live together happily.

There are, of course, many creative ways to make things work if both parties are invested in a solution. I've seen couples where the man is a minimalist, and most of the house reflects this until you go into the woman's craft room which is overflowing from every cabinet with brightly colored craft supplies! Looking at the end tables on both sides of their bed, there was also no question of whose space was whose. But I've also seen where the man was so rigid in his "model home" aesthetic that a neat pile on an end table consisting of a book, organizer, and a notepad caused heated arguments and deep-seated resentment. Both people deserve to feel like they can live within their homes in a way that they enjoy.

Workspace:

Shifting between the Home space and Work space, I

found a well-supported article written by Louise Delagran for the University of Minnesota. The study speaks about the importance of a healthy personal environment. Here are her top tips for facilitating both a healthy home and workspace.

"How Does Your Personal Environment Impact Your Well-being?"

"Your home and work environment can:

• Influence your mood. For example, research studies reveal that rooms with bright light, both natural and artificial, can improve depression and anxiety.

• Impact your behavior and motivation to act. For example, a messy hall with shoes, bags, and other stuff may invite you to drop what you are carrying right there, whereas a clean entry and adequate storage will encourage you to take the time to put the item away.

• Facilitate or discourage interactions in your family and with guests. For example, an inviting space with comfortable chairs can encourage people to sit and chat.

. . .

• *Create or reduce stress, which impacts not only your emotional but also physical health, including your longevity!" -Louise Delagran, MA, MEd*

-https://www.takingcharge.csh.umn.edu/how-does-your-personal-environment-impact-your-wellbeing

There might be a slight resistance to the idea of making changes at work because some people feel that there's no way a boss would go for it. You might be surprised by their response. They need to exist in that workspace, also.

If you have a boss that isn't interested in your thoughts and ideas, then... I'm here to remind you that life is short. Too short to live an unfulfilling life. So if your work does not promote well-being, then it might be time to reconsider where you work. You wouldn't want to date a man who's miserable working their job, so why should you be?

I can tell you from first-hand experience that ever since I became an independent author, my life has improved by leaps and bounds! That's not what this book is about, so I'll keep this thought super short. Being self-employed or freelancing has improved my life and the lives of many of my friends significantly.

Ok, there, now I can sleep better tonight if that helps even one person.

Free-time spaces:

Just because the environment is beautiful, it doesn't mean it's where you should be spending your time. Focus on how it supports a feeling of actual well-being. Remember that is the all-important focus.

This reminds me of a story of a man who was spending his vacations golfing. No matter where in the world he was, he would always schedule a tee time and head out to the golf course. Well, one day, he was in a sand trap, sweating and cursing as he tried to get back on track, and he had an epiphany. "What am I doing? I'm stressed out, I'm sweating, and I'm miserable! Why am I here? This isn't relaxing at all." He left the golf course and went to the beach and got a Piña Colada. Problem solved. Now on every vacation he takes, he no longer schedules golf time. Instead, he asks himself what activity would nourish him so that when he goes back to work, he feels recharged.

So take another look at how you spend your free time. Is it filling you full of positive emotions of some kind? Is it actually restoring you and nurturing you on some level? If not, then why are you still doing it? It's your free time's job to make you feel better, so make sure it's earning the time you give it.

Mr. Right's Physical Spaces

Looking at the physical environment that the man of your dreams inhabits will tell you an incredible amount about him. For example, if he has a job that involves working outdoors, that shows that he most likely values the feeling of freedom. Either that or he may love the grounding feeling of working with his hands and being connected with the land. It's important to ask what he loves about the physical environment of his workplace. I doubt anyone's ever asked him.

My husband Liam had never been asked about this physical work environment before me, and he was fascinated when I asked him. He told me that the questions I asked on our dates really stuck with him and made him reflect. He appreciated the "8 Dimensions of Wellness" and we had a long discussion about both big and little things that really bring us joy. This is an example of how well this type of discussion will go with someone who is interested in building a life with you.

Guys who are interested in the long term need a lot of information, and guys who are only interested in the short term only need a little information, which they can gather very quickly, usually in the form of a not-subtle look up and down. This isn't to say that a guy should be asking tons of questions on the first date. He might want to get a feel for your energy and see what your natural inclinations are before he really starts investigating further. As long as he doesn't try to avoid these types of discussions and take it back to surface levels consistently, you're in the clear.

Timing: Be sure to time things correctly. Seeing how a man lives in the privacy of his own home isn't generally first date material. There are so many interesting things to get to know about a potential partner that this is one that often can wait, and that's ok! Asking him about his work environment during a romantic stroll through a garden could probably also be better timing. He might feel like you're not actually in the moment and, by extension, not appreciating his efforts to court you. We don't want to waste unnecessary time but don't forget that this is a human being that you are getting to know. Try to enjoy the process and let things progress naturally.

Dating Examples: Environmental
Choosing unhappiness, guy.

I met a guy on a popular dating app. He was handsome and funny, and his banter was incredibly engaging. I was really enjoying him on a video chat, so I agreed to drinks. He was a bartender by trade, so I was extra excited to get a drink with him because bartenders always have some hidden gems of mixology to share.

He said we could meet for a quick drink, or he'd have to wait again until next week because his workweek hours didn't work for a date. That could be a "physical" or "occupational" dimension issue, but I thought I'd meet him anyway.

He was absolutely lovely on the date. We laughed all night. I tried some fun new drinks, and he was a complete gentleman all evening. "Wow, I really like him. We'll have to see where this goes." I thought to myself on my way home. By the time I got home, he had already texted me and invited me to his bar for a special drink the next night. I accepted.

I showed up the next night at the bar, and it was... depressing. The bar had a distinctly gloomy vibe to it despite the festive-looking Tiki decorations throughout the bar. He was dressed in a Hawaiian shirt that looked happy and bright, but he looked depleted. I chalked it up to him having a rough night.

He made me his signature drink which was delicious. He talked to me as much as he could, but he was at work, and I didn't have any expectations of spending quality time together. That wasn't the issue. The issue was that I watched his face while he worked, and he looked miserable. Mixing drinks, ringing the bell when someone gave him a tip, keeping conversations going with strangers, none of it looked like he cared for it at all. "Maybe this isn't the career for him," I thought to myself. I told him I was going to head home, and he asked me if I'd come to see him tomorrow night at a friend's bar he was working at. He said he wanted some feedback about the place because they had just started serving food, and they needed an honest opinion on the chef they hired. I thought, "Ok, why not?"

The next night rolled around, and I showed up at this fun gastropub that had an upbeat and energetic vibe to it. My date was mixing drinks and serving them, except this time, he was vibrant and lit up with happiness. I ordered some food and gave my feedback. It was delicious.

I told him that he seems so much happier here; why doesn't he work here with his friend full-time? He said that he had been with the other bar for a long time and that he knew the owner there, and he had some great insurance. Well, good insurance in the United States is extremely important, but he was making tons of tips at his friend's bar so he could buy great insurance. More importantly, though, he was happy!

He told me that he couldn't just leave the other bar hanging because he was the most popular bartender there, and without him, the place probably wouldn't be doing as well. Well, that's a noble stance but isn't your happiness worth something to you? He told me I didn't get it. Agreed. It's not like he was best friends with the Tiki bar owner, but he was best friends with this fantastic new gastropub owner.

I asked him directly,
Me: "Are you happy at the Tiki bar?"
Him: "Come on. It's not that bad."
Me: "That's not the best, is it?"
Him: "Like I said, you don't get it."
Me: "True. You're so happy here. You know what? My sincere apologies. It's none of my business. It's just fun to see you have a good time with your friend. Let's leave it at that."
Him: "Yeah, I mean, sometimes you gotta do what you gotta do, right?"

Those last words are poisonous in my world. They are

the opposite of magic and chasing down dreams. So not only was he choosing an environment that was making him miserable for some reason, but he was also letting on that he had a core belief that would affect other dimensions as well.

Key Takeaways from this interaction

1. Life is about choices. If you look at the choices that someone is making consistently in their life and they don't make sense to you, then that person probably doesn't make sense for you as a partner.

2. Loyalty is admirable but how he applied loyalty in his day to day life had negative effects on him. This was also echoed in other areas of his life. Looking for patterns of behavior is like a crystal ball into the future!

3. The long-term effects of his choices and how he applied his values would definitely affect any relationship we could have together. These speak to core values and core values affect every decision and aspect of life.

Reflection:
So what feelings come up when you think of your home space, work space and free time spaces? How

would you describe them to someone who's never seen them? Not in architectural terms or anything a realtor would use to describe it. What positive feelings do these spaces share? Are there negative feelings that are associated with any or all of them? Take a pen or pencil out and answer below...

Home Space:

How does it currently feel?

How would you like it to feel?

What changes, if any, need to be made?

What type of person would you want to wake up in the morning next to? Be the last person you spoke to before going to bed at night? Spend an entire weekend at home with?

How was that experience? Were you surprised at your responses, or is that where you thought you were? Either way, clarity is an excellent thing in life. When defining our home space, we need to think specifically about its impact on our well-being.

Now let's move on to our workspace. If you're already

thinking back to the Occupational Dimension from chapter 2, then my hats off to you. This time instead of thinking about the culture of your workspace or your coworkers, we're looking at the physical environment by itself. So thinking objectively about the physical environment, what emotions come up?

Work Space:

How does it currently feel?

How would you like it to feel?

What changes can be made?

What type of person do you want waiting for you when you get home from work or sitting next to you if you both work from home?

Now let's take a look at our free time space. What's the physical environment in which you choose to spend your downtime? Do you have a place that you enjoy going on the weekends? How does this environment support your well-being?

Free time Space:

How does it currently feel?

How would you like it to feel?

What changes, if any, need to be made?

What type of person makes this experience even more enjoyable?

Your free time space should be replenishing for your mind, body, and soul. If it's not ticking those boxes, then why on Earth are you giving it your precious time?

How this goes on your list:

Take a look back at your "Reflection" notes in this chapter. Are you seeing certain themes repeated? Maybe you want a bohemian space with a zen vibe? Perhaps sleek cosmopolitan spaces are more your speed? Or rustic settings surrounded by nature?

What are the traits of the man you can see standing by your side in these environments? Which of these traits are imperative to your happiness?

Potential Environmental Dimension "Must-Haves":

1.

2.

3.

Maybe you've noticed that nowhere in this chapter have we discussed the square footage of the house you'd like to live in. Personally, I would rather be in an impeccably decorated tiny home with someone whose company I enjoy every moment of (Liam) than in a mansion that is empty of love and laughter.

As always, I am wishing all my Brilliant Vixen's the best of both worlds, whatever that may look like for you!

Brilliant Vixen Secret Bonus #4: Environmental, aka Fun Ways to Meet Mr. Right using the Environmental Dimension!

For this bonus, it's all about being aware when you're at a store that focuses on making at least one of your environments better.

Pay attention to the men around when spending time in stores that focus on home improvement. This is not to say you hang out at a lumber yard waiting for a contractor who looks like he'd be happy to build you a new bathroom.

What I'm talking about is if you're at a home organization store or if you're taking a Feng Shui or Hygge class, take a look around. The guys are clearly actively working on improving at least one of their spaces.

Admittedly the majority of single guys won't be learning about Feng Shui. They'll be buying bike racks, storage bins, or barbecues (I love it when it's BBQ time), but that's still a guy who cares about his environment and wants it to be more comfortable.

Guys who are spending time thinking about their environments are thinking men. These types of men are constantly striving to make things a little better. Even if it's something small, they're not just leaving things as good enough. They want their worlds to evolve in at least some small way over time. This leads directly into the next dimension of wellness.

Chapter Five

INTELLECTUAL

I have no special talent. I am only passionately curious."
-Albert Einstein

This is definitely not about a person's IQ level. This dimension is about your intellectual pursuits, including recognizing your unique creative abilities. This also deals with one of the principles found in "The 7 Essential Elements of Irresistible Women". Chapter 7 is "Constantly Evolving." Which deals with the importance of continuing to learn and better yourself.

"Engaging in creative, mentally stimulating activities, and being curious about the world are key components of your Intellectual Wellness."
   - Northwestern.edu

When talking to my daughter Janis about finding people to spend time with, we stress how important it is for someone to be curious about the world and open to learning. Without any curiosity about the world, people become inflexible and detached from life itself to some degree. We've summarized this as "Are they too cool for...?"

A person who is "Too cool for..." has made a conscious decision not even to attempt to learn anything new. They turn their nose up at new experiences or the chance to gain further insight. They're choosing to be stagnant in their thinking which, especially in their later years, will substantially increase the likelihood of being stubborn and inflexible.

Intellectual pursuits can be anything that stimulates the mind with learning. More traditional examples of this would be a lecture on philosophical thought or history. But I would encourage you to open your mind to the idea that learning about anything that interests you has value. It keeps the mind young and agile. You could learn about how the DC Universe differs from the Marvel universe or how different types of paddles help kayaks move more quickly through the water. What you or your potential partner choose to learn says a lot about who you are as a person. Choosing not to actively learn at all also says quite a bit about who you are and how you feel about life.

"Everything that you experience leaves its mark on your brain. When you learn something new, the neurons involved in the learning episode grow new projections and form new connections. Your brain may even produce new neurons."

https://elifesciences.org/digests/52743/how-experience-shapes-the-brain

The most exciting form of intellectual well-being that I've encountered is a playful curiosity about life. A passion for continually evolving as a person keeps us fascinating to those around us. Just think about it like a school reunion. What do you say to the person who's exactly the same as they were when you left school? Not much, really. You have a few nice pleasantries and maybe rehash some old memories, then that's it. There's really not that much more to talk about. Whereas the person who's been working on themselves ever since you left school is fascinating, and you could talk to them all night. Now imagine a lifetime of conversations or lack thereof. How much fuller does that lifetime feel if you are both constantly evolving and sharing new interests, information and experiences with each other?

One of the things that attracted me to my husband, Liam, was that when I asked him an intellectual question, he would smile and think about it before responding. That's all the information I needed before he even answered. He demonstrated playful curiosity from the moment I asked the question.

Liam is a very masculine man, but his playful curiosity will take him outside traditional roles from time to time. For example, my sister was devastated that her best friend, who was supposed to throw her a baby shower, called a week before the baby shower and said she couldn't do it. Liam smiled and said, "I'll do it." to which we both fell silent in disbelief. He continued, "Yeah, why not? You guys are both busy already. I'll figure it out. It'll be fun." My sister was equally relieved and concerned all over again. Liam spent hours researching what kinds of activities were often done at baby showers and came up with some hilarious games for the attendees to play. He even came up with the now infamous "Golden Baby Award"! Those spray-painted little plastic babies on Mardi Gras beads were a highly coveted prize. Long story short, he killed it! The baby shower was a huge hit, and my sister's friends raved about how much fun they had. The point is Liam was showing a playful curiosity and a willingness to learn, both of which demonstrate high intellectual well-being.

"Creativity is Intelligence having fun."
    -Albert Einstein

When people say, "We just grew apart," I often find that the reality is that one person continued to evolve and grow while the other remained stagnant. In my personal experience, men who avoid fostering any intellectual pursuits are incredibly dull. They don't learn new things or develop as a person over the years. They just age. Unfortunately, I have a perfect example of a date that demonstrated this to perfection.

Dating Examples: Intellectual
Like, what do you mean, guy?

I met a guy on a popular dating app, not the swiping kind, to be precise. He seemed very down to Earth and normal when we first started talking, so I thought, why not go out for a meal and see if there's any chemistry there? We arrived at a fantastic Gastro pub in the Art District of Las Vegas and got seated. He looked exactly like he did in his profile which is always good. He had an athletic build, upbeat energy and was good-looking. Ok, those are all nice things, but let's see what he's all about.

Everything seemed to be going reasonably well until we got to the intellectual dimension. I asked him a question that apparently he'd never been asked before in his dating life, which was quite a surprise to me as it seemed pretty standard.

"So, what do you like to do?" I asked. His response was one that there was no way I could've predicted. He said his beer down and looked at me like I was a literal ghost. In reality, I'm sure less than a second had passed since I asked the question, but it felt like an eternity.

His demeanor was as though I had just asked him if he wanted to have kids after dessert. His response was cautious, to say the least. He very slowly said, "Like, what do you mean?" As though this was a trick question and the answer would immediately get him kicked off the island.

I smiled to ease his tension. I let out a little laugh and said, "I mean, what do you like to do when you're not working or on dates?" I thought that explanation was more than enough to clear up any confusion that might've inadvertently happened. I was giving him the benefit of the doubt that maybe he thought I was trying to sneakily find out what he did for a living and exactly how much money he made. That's not an uncommon mistake for women to make, after all.

He took a quick look around the room, which I

found interesting before he proceeded to say very cautiously: "Well, I know the bartender over there, so I come here and get some drinks." I smiled and nodded to encourage him to keep going, and he skittishly obliged. "And, uh...I also go to the gym every day, and you know, kick back and grab some beers with the Bros." I continued to smile and tried to make him more comfortable. "Ok, well, it's good to stay active. And it's nice to have a good group of friends to socialize with." He still seemed very cautious, like he was formulating exactly how he was going to tell his friends about the nightmare questions I was asking him after the date.

I think just to take the focus off himself; he said, "Well, what do you do?" I told him I had taken up working with hot glass and making beads. I had previously had an amazing mentor who introduced me to glass blowing. He was a retired NASA rocket scientist who just wanted to do art full-time now. I told him I thought it was cool that even after all that guy had accomplished that he still was looking for things that were entirely new for him to experiment with and that we're never too old to stop growing as people.

I thought maybe that response intimidated him a little because he got extra quiet, so I followed it up with, "Yeah, he knows a ton about space, but when you start talking about what the latest movie was about, he has no idea what I'm talking about! But he's still curious." My date was still quietly drinking his beer, so I tried to ask him an even easier question. "So, what's your favorite movie?" He responded with the same cautious look and "I don't really go to movies. I just like to work out. Sometimes they have movie nights on here, though," he said as he motioned towards the big screen above the bar.

He let out a big sigh and flexed his biceps, making sure I saw it. A bemused smile crept onto my face as I thought "Is it really possible that this is the entirety of who this guy is?" He then smiled and looked at me in his best seductive way. "So you want to get out of here and come check out my apartment?" he said while raising an eyebrow. The smile immediately left my face. "Oh no, I'm definitely not that kind of girl." The smile left his face. "Oh, um, ok?" He questioned, sitting back in his chair, pouting. I asked for the check, and we went our separate ways.

Key Takeaways from this interaction

1. This man was beyond stuck in a rut. He was functioning on such extreme auto-pilot that he found my innocent question about what he liked to do bizarre.

2. His responses showed a lack of intellectual pursuits in any area.

3. There was no future for me with someone who had already quit growing or having curiosity about life at such a young age.

Funny Epilogue:

Several years later, I was at the same Gastropub with close friends and family, celebrating my Bachelor/Bachelorette party with Liam. On the way up the stairs, guess who hadn't moved an inch? The same guy! Liam passed him on the staircase and obviously had no idea who he was. When I passed him he looked at me and smiled from ear to ear saying, "Hey, what's up? I haven't seen you in a while! Wanna grab a drink?" I kept walking up the stairs and turned to say a few words on my way up.

I couldn't contain a smile as I looked at him and said, "No, I don't think that's a very good idea." I pointed to the enormous necklace I was wearing that said "bride-to-be" and my hat that said "getting married." He looked at both of those, and his jaw just hung there wide open. I broke off the interaction with a "Good luck!" Just then, Liam noticed the exchange and asked what that was all about. I had told Liam this story before and let him know that that was the same guy from the infamous "So what do you like to do" date. Liam laughed and said, "And this is the same place you had that date in?" I smiled and said, "yup." Liam shook his head and laughed, "Wow! Well, he's definitely consistent. I'll give him that much." Then we turned and continued up the stairs. I would say that I couldn't believe he was in exactly the same place doing exactly the same thing so many years later, but when I thought about it, that's the precise reason that I wasn't interested all those years before. I wanted a life that grew and changed while he was very clearly content exactly where he was.

Reflection:

"The day we stop playing will be the day we stop learning."
— William Glasser

What kind of intellectual pursuits do you enjoy? What do you have a playful curiosity about? What kind of learning feels like playing to you?

What kind of creativity do you find attractive? Is it

creative ways to solve practical problems? Artistic creativity? Creative ways to make or save money?

What kinds of activities do you find mentally stimulating? Learning a new climbing route up a mountain? Listening to an author speak about their book? Learning about the history of a new place you're visiting?

How this goes on your list:

Take a look at your reflection notes and really think about the type of man who would enjoy learning about similar things as you. What kind of person would creatively come up with activities you would enjoy together? Ultimately what kind of person would you still find fascinating as you hold hands on your 50th wedding anniversary?

Potential Intellectual Dimension "Must-Haves":

1.

2.

3.

Brilliant Vixen Secret Bonus #5: Intellectual aka Fun Ways to Meet Mr. Right using the Intellectual Dimension!

My husband Liam was in high school, and he was chasing a girl that he fancied. One day she said she had signed up for a rock-climbing retreat and asked if hc wanted to come along. He thought about it and decided, why not? He went and discovered that he loved rock climbing! So much so that he became a professional rock climbing guide and even prepared athletes for trips to Mount Everest. So in his pursuit of this girl, combined with a playful curiosity about the world, he discovered something incredible about himself. That discovery had a significant impact on his life, and it's all because he kept a curious mind. He could have easily told the girl he'd see her when she returned, but he didn't and decided to go outside his comfort zone.

I don't recommend chasing men, but if one presents an opportunity to try something new (and, of course, doesn't put you in any situation that makes you legitimately uncomfortable), you should strongly consider it. You might be like Liam and discover an activity you adore, even if the date doesn't work out.

The bonus for this section is this. Make time to

explore things that you're curious about. Pick an activity that lets your intellect run wild and play. When you follow that playfulness, you can connect with others that are in the same place. What's something you've always wanted to try but haven't made time for? Just remember, if it's a positive activity, it can lead to a quality man.

When you let your mind take the lead and start exploring your curiosities, it will breathe new life into you. It has the potential to change everything, and for me, this method has led me to more incredible places than I could ever imagine. Most people would never put these two together, but intelligence keeps magic alive.

All this magic will put you around a whole lot of new people, which leads right into our next dimension.

Chapter Six

SOCIAL

"*A deep sense of love and belonging is an irreducible need of all people. We are biologically, cognitively, physically, and spiritually wired to love, to be loved, and to belong. When those needs are not met, we don't function as we were meant to. We break. We fall apart. We numb. We ache. We hurt others. We get sick.*" *-Brene Brown.*

This next dimension deals with connection and belonging. It definitely has zero to do with how many followers you have on social media. That's a whole other can of worms. If you are feeling lonely please know that you are not alone in this. In a recent survey sponsored by The Cigna Health Insurance Company, 46% of respondents reported sometimes or always feeling alone. Social media has actually been shown to contribute to higher levels of loneliness, anxiety and depression. We are going to be looking at ways to increase social wellness during this chapter, both on our own and with a potential partner.

"Social wellness is defined as developing a sense of connection, belonging, and a well-developed support system."

https://www.northwestern.edu/wellness/8-dimensions/social-wellness.html

"Signs of Social Wellness

• *Development of assertiveness skills, not passive or aggressive ones.*
• *Balancing social and personal time.*
• *The ability to be who you are in all situations.*
• *Becoming engaged with other people in your community.*
• *Valuing diversity and treat(ing) others with respect.*
• *Continually being able to maintain and develop friendships and social networks.*
• *The ability to create boundaries within relationship(s,)*

boundaries that encourage communication, trust and conflict
management.
• Remembering to have fun.
• Having (a) supportive network of family and friends."

-https://www.unh.edu/health/social-wellness

Do you have a support network? What does it consist of? Does your support network only include people on payroll like a therapist (a great therapist is invaluable btw!), the hair stylist that you confide in, employees etc.? Or is your support network a mix of people on payroll plus friends and family?

Do you have any communities you feel connected to? Perhaps an art cooperative, a book club, a place of worship or a sports team?

I think most people have phases of their life where their social circle is not as well rounded as they would like and I can speak from experience that families can be complicated. There are definitely members of my family I don't include in my support network because they're not willing/able to be supportive. I've also upgraded some of my long-term friends to the "family" category, and they've been a massive part of my support network.

"It is not just receiving support but also giving support that can boost well-being. In a study using a sample of a quarter million people from 136 countries, Aknin and Dunn (2013) found that spending money on others paid back dividends. Of note, spending on others was associated with greater levels of well-being than comparable purchases spent on oneself."

-Diener, Ed, et al. *Social Well-Being: Research and Policy Recommendations.*

That being said, some people are happier in a larger social circle, and some thrive in a smaller one, but the trope of the lone wolf should be left to the big screen. Wolves actually have complex social structures, and they draw their power from their pack. A lone wolf is at a marked disadvantage from the protection of belonging to a pack. Human beings are also better suited to belonging, and studies show that, quite often, loners suffer significant emotional distress. There is no such thing as a wolf pack of one.

"We cannot separate the importance of a sense of belonging from our physical and mental health. The social ties that accompany a sense of belonging are a protective factor helping manage stress and other behavioral issues. When we feel we have support and are not alone, we are more resilient, often coping more effectively with difficult times in our lives. Coping well with hardships decreases the physical and mental effects of these situations."

-Angela Theisen, Psychotherapist in Psychiatry & Psychology for Mayo Clinic

The ability to form solid friendships doesn't always come easily and can require quite a bit of time and energy, but the end result is worth the effort! Remember all those Secret Bonus sections? The good news is that those sections are equally good at helping you grow your social circle. If you are using those sections correctly, then you will be making time for your favorite activities or finding new ones you truly enjoy. Connecting over shared interests is one of the easiest ways to make new friends. The advice of walking up to someone and asking a question about the current activity is just as likely to yield a platonic as a romantic connection. That's ok because these connections are all beneficial to your overall sense of happiness!

Now it's possible that you've been reading this section and saying, "My friend group is absolutely amazing and completely supportive!" Well, then, I commend you because it will be even easier to see how a potential partner will fit into your life.

I have a very dear friend who has a vibrant and healthy social circle. She is active in several communities, works, and still finds time to volunteer for charity organizations. She's an amazing human being and it's more than a little surprising that she's still single! Her Prince Charming will need to be someone who fits into all or most of her activities though. Now that may seem like a negative but in fact it's a wonderful way to test for compatibility. Would you really want to have a partner in life who doesn't enjoy any of the same things as you do?

Whether you are adding to your social circle or starting from scratch, take some time to think about how your connections, both romantic and platonic, will fit into your life. It is rare that these connections don't need to overlap and fit together in some way.

Dating Example: Social

The Lone Wolf

I met this gentleman at an art fair in a park. He was selling some beautiful paintings of landscapes. I found the paintings incredibly captivating, and he caught my eye as well.

He approached me, and naturally, we struck up a conversation about his artistic viewpoint and his work in general. One thing led to another, and he invited me on a date. He was an interesting guy, brooding and artistically gifted. I was very excited to see his take on the world.

Date night came, and we met at a small locals-only cafe. We ordered some coffee and small plates, and it was very relaxing. His views on life and the arts did not disappoint. He was very soulful. He saw the artistic merit in everything, how beauty was waiting to be discovered in most things if you look hard enough. It was a lovely evening.

Things didn't start to unravel until we reached social

wellness topics. He didn't have any contact with his parents. In Las Vegas, I find that many people don't have much of a relationship with at least one of their parents, so it wasn't entirely out of the norm. But both parents? It was a little unusual, but it's possible that there are valid and healthy reasons for this.

We got onto the topic of friends, and he nodded patiently as I described my friend group. When I asked about what his best friend was like, he replied, "I don't really hang out with a lot of people. There are a few guys from the art fair who are cool, and sometimes I see them at functions, but I wouldn't really call them my friends."

That was more concerning to me. No real friends? That made me really uncomfortable. Now thinking back to the comment about his parents, I saw a substantial lone-wolf pattern.

Our discussion shifted to what to do around the holidays, and he told me he liked to take advantage of all the sales but as far as celebrating, it wasn't really his thing. He enjoyed traveling outside the United States because all the trips to the places he went were cheaper, even if the flights were a little crowded.

That was the last straw for me. He wasn't a bad guy

by any stretch of the imagination, but this wasn't for me at all. I love the holidays. A big part of the holidays is having traditions that involve loved ones. I like baking for my friends and family. I love watching cheesy holiday movies all bundled up with a hot chocolate in our hands.

It's the interaction with people that make all the celebrations in life special to me. He didn't share those values. In fact, he thought the idea was a little antiquated.

Definitely not my type of guy. I needed people in my life, and he felt that he didn't. Simple as that.

Key Takeaways from this interaction

You can learn a ton about people from what their social circle looks like.

1. He had no close connections of any kind, which means that he didn't see the value in maintaining long-term relationships with people. That didn't speak well for his desire or ability to maintain a long-term romantic relationship either.

2. I saw that this viewpoint was so at odds with the

way I view life that we were completely incompatible.

Reflection

I think most of us have had a time where we had either more or fewer friends than our norm. I certainly have had times when my support system was very light. It's normal for there to be variations due to circumstances. I would like you to think about when you were the happiest in your friend circle and also how you felt when you weren't happy with your social circumstances. What kind of people make you feel happy and relaxed? What type helps you feel inspired and intellectually stimulated? Do you have the willingness and desire to get out of your comfort zone if it's time to grow your circle?

When you start dating, you can take a look at whether he has what you would consider a well-balanced and healthy social life. He doesn't have to be the mayor, but he should have formed quality relationships by the time he's an adult. If he hasn't, then that's a huge red flag that something more concerning is just below the surface.

Does he have close friends and family? Are they the type of people you can see yourself spending time with? Does he treat them in a way that shows that he cares for them?

Does he have a healthy-feeling social community that you can see yourself enjoying? Does he treat them in a way that shows that he values them?

What are his best friends like? How does he treat them? That is a huge barometer of who he really is and what he truly values.

How this goes on your list:

As you start to or continue to grow your circle, it is very possible that you will meet a potential romantic partner. Sometimes having a partner to grow your circle with can be a fantastic confidence booster, but it is important to look at this person and consider whether they are the type of person who you will be proud to have by your side in social situations. Now, I definitely don't mean that you should worry about whether they are impressive to other people on a surface level. I mean, are you proud of how they treat other people? Of how they treat you? Of their morals and values? If this is not a person who you would be excited to introduce to your current friends or to make new ones with, then the reasons why deserve some careful consideration.

You should think about the qualities that you value. If you look at your support network, do they share traits that you would also want in a partner? Do you highly value directness and honesty? Tact? A fantastic sense of humor? Is it important that your partner has a certain level of sociability? Or that they are comfortable in certain groups? Are there traits that help you feel cared for, supported or like you belong?

Potential Social Dimension "Must-Haves":

1.

2.

3.

Brilliant Vixen Secret Bonus #6: Social

In an effort to expand our Social Wellness Dimension, we need to first check in with ourselves. When we look at our support network, it will tell us if we need to expand it or strengthen it if it's not helping us properly. We shouldn't count people who aren't actually helping us thrive in life. If someone never really offers supportive words or it seems like they're bothered by listening, then they aren't part of your support network. That doesn't mean they are not good people. It's just that they can't serve that role for you.

Let's also check in on the communities you're involved in. Are they healthy for you emotionally? Is the culture in that community one that nourishes you? Are there any other communities you might also be interested in that could provide better connections or a better support system for you? Are there communities that you could provide value to? In order to be socially well, you must contribute to, as well as benefit from, your social connections.

So once you've checked in with the healthiness of your current social circle, then you can move on to the fun stuff.

Forming new healthy relationships and growing existing solid and healthy relationships in your network can unlock new worlds for you. These new worlds can also include quality men. Let's say you really hit it off with a girl in one of the Secret Bonus activities that you're trying for one of your other wellness dimensions. This new friend invites you to check out an event that none of your other friends would be interested in. That new event is brimming with men who share your interests. Now because you have a new friend to attend these different events with, your social dimension just unlocked a whole new group of men. Not only that, but you have a trusty wing-woman at your side with whom you can discuss the men you encounter.

New friends may also have people they can introduce you to and tell you who is single before you even say hello. They might even already have the wheels turning on who they know would be a perfect match for you. Let's look out for one another, ladies. If there's a great guy you know that would be perfect for one of your single friends, don't be shy to mention him.

So with those strategies in mind, let's move onto an extremely telling dimension that reveals an incredible amount of information about a potential romantic interest. Emotions.

Chapter Seven

EMOTIONAL

"Today I choose life. Every morning when I wake up I can choose joy, happiness, negativity, pain... To feel the freedom that comes from being able to continue to make mistakes and choices - today I choose to feel life, not to deny my humanity but embrace it." -Kevyn Aucoin

Emotional compatibility is very important in a romantic relationship, but before we can take a look at compatibility, we need to first check in on emotional wellness.

Emotional Wellness is your ability to cope with life stress, express your emotions in healthy ways and feel positive about life. It includes being self-aware enough to see the areas where you could practice self-improvement but also be able to recognize your strengths. Being emotionally well allows you to communicate your feelings with others and create healthy connections.

Let's start by taking a little more in-depth look at those points one by one.

Ability to cope with life's stress:

It is perfectly natural, normal, and indeed fairly unavoidable to feel emotions like anger, anxiety and fear. It is our ways of coping with emotions like these that indicate our state of emotional wellness. When we are angry, do we lash out at others in physically violent or emotionally destructive ways? Or do we use the energy of anger to set healthy boundaries or right injustice?

When we feel anxiety, do we work on finding the root cause, so we know whether action or acceptance is necessary? Or do we put the full weight of our problems on others and expect them to magically fix them for us? When we are fearful, do we resort to anger and violence? Do we hide from our problems and hope they'll go away? Or do we reach out in healthy ways for support? Being able to cope with life's stress does not mean that you can or should do it all alone. A supportive friend or a trusted therapist can be invaluable when it comes to navigating life. Knowing when to reach out is a sign of emotional strength, not weakness!

Express your emotions in healthy ways:

While researching this book, I found that, yes, even Buddhist monks feel anger. So it's what we do when the inevitable happens that really matters! Do we take a deep breath and then wait to communicate until we have cleared our head? Or do we hurl physical or emotional destruction in the direction that the perceived offense came from? Whether that's the TV, another driver on the road, or our romantic partner. I believe that there are no inherently "bad" emotions, just unhealthy ways of expressing them.

Take love, for example. An emotion that should be "good," yet I have seen people use it to suffocate, guilt and stifle their supposed "loved one." Or sadness, a supposed "bad" emotion. I have seen it used to express a healthy mourning period for a loss. It can be a catalyst for change, or it can simply help you slow down for a moment to reevaluate life. It is not in the labels of our emotions that we will find whether we are emotionally well. It is in how they affect our lives and the lives of those around us.

Feel positively about life:

This is not to say that every moment of every day should be spent skipping through a field of daisies. I mean, yes, after saying that, I now really want to skip through a field of daisies! What this really means in terms of emotional wellness is that you generally have positive feelings about living. There are things that you enjoy in your day-to-day life, and there are things you are looking forward to in your future. Now some people are naturally more optimistic, and others lean more towards pessimistic views, but contrary to popular belief, people aren't just one or the other.

One study states that "Successful living requires a fine balance between optimism and pessimism." This same study found that a belief in external locus of control (your life is controlled by outside forces) promoted pessimism, while beliefs about internal locus of control (your actions influence your reality) promoted an increase in optimism. Basically, they found that simply writing an essay about a time when your actions positively influenced the outcome of a situation could increase optimism and that the effects were lasting. I think that the fact that you're taking the time to read this book and do the work it entails speaks volumes about your willingness and ability to influence your reality with your decisions.

Self-aware enough to see the areas where you could practice self-improvement but also be able to recognize your strengths:

Do you have a healthy and realistic view of yourself? Since you're here doing the work in this book you likely don't have problems practicing self-improvement. A narcissist wouldn't still be here as they're quite sure they're already perfect. Nobody's perfect but do you give yourself credit for where you're amazing? Do you recognize your mistakes but still practice kindness to yourself?

Speaking of being kind to yourself, what's your self-talk like? The way we talk to ourselves says a lot about our emotional health.

Here's how I like to put negative self-talk into perspective. Would I talk to my best friend like that? Then why is it ok to talk to me like that? If it's really such "constructive criticism," then why wouldn't I say it to my friend in the same way that I'm saying it to myself? Here's a hidden secret about a well-known saying. The golden rule applies to you too. So treat yourself the way you want to be treated also.

I want to raise my hand and admit that my self-talk needs improvement, and I'm working on making that change. As I write this, I'm on a little hot streak of actually being nice to myself. That's a nice bonus to writing self-help books for a living. You learn so much about taking care of yourself in the process of writing about caring for others.

I discovered that not only does negative self-talk damage our emotional well-being, but it goes all the way back to the first dimension and damages our physical well-being.

"According to Paul Gilbert, who created compassion-focused therapy (CFT), when we criticize ourselves, we're tapping into the body's threat-defense system (some- times referred to as our reptilian brain). Among the many ways we can react to perceived danger, the threat-defense system is the quickest and most easily triggered. This means that self-criticism is often our first reaction when things go wrong....Feeling threatened puts stress on the

> *mind and body, and chronic stress can cause*
> *anxiety and depression, which is why habitual*
> *self-criticism is so bad for emotional and physical*
> *well-being. With self-criticism, we are both the*
> *attacker and the attacked."*- Neff, K. & Germer,
> C. (2018). The Mindful Self-Compassion
> Workbook: A Proven Way to Accept Yourself,
> Build Inner Strength, and Thrive.

Cutting down on criticizing myself has been no easy task, and it certainly doesn't mean that I've stopped trying to improve. I'm just talking to myself in healthier ways, and the rewards are already great.

So now that we've discussed how you talk to yourself let's take a look at the kind of person that you enjoy talking to when you're navigating life's challenges. Do you have one or more specific people in mind that have been invaluable in their support of you? What character traits do they possess? If it's more than one person, are those traits similar to each other? Are they emotionally even-keeled, free of judgment, full of great advice, a great listener, optimistic or empathetic? Perhaps you have had friends or family who were supportive in some ways but a romantic partner who was supportive in other ways?

There is more than one way for someone to be emotionally supportive of you. Sometimes it's them being emotionally strong for you, and other times it's them being strong enough to be emotionally vulnerable with you.

Although it is crucial that you are able to discuss life's challenges with a romantic partner, it is also unfair for you to expect one person to be your only source of emotional support. There is a difference between emotional support and emotional dependence.

Healthy boundaries are essential to emotional independence.

"Emotional independence is a type of inner resilience that lets you know you can meet, solve, and be with any circumstance you face. It means building your sense of self on your own, without depending on others to make you happy or tell you who you should be."

-Strauss Cohen, Ilene. "How to Live an Emotionally Independent Life | Psychology Today."

Without proper boundaries, we get pushed around and ultimately end up in a place that's entirely out of our control. We all have known someone who's an emotional doormat, and it's their complete lack of boundaries that makes them miserable. Boundaries are a powerful form of self-love and need to be respected. Maybe it seems counterintuitive to talk about emotional independence in a dating book where we're looking for love, but if you are searching for love outside yourself and you haven't found it inside yourself first, then you are starting at a deficit and expecting someone else to fill it.

Ok, we've taken a nice overview of how we can check in with ourselves about our emotional well-being. Now let's see how that relates to the hunt for Mr. Right. There are some simple ways to start to gauge his emotional wellness, even on a first date!

Surprisingly some of these are so clear that even over the phone or a text, you just can't miss them if you're looking for them.

Ability to cope with life's stress:

Have you seen him solve stressful problems in a healthy way? Or have you seen signs of anger or irritation that you don't find to be equitable to the problem at hand? Has he mentioned healthy ways he "blows off steam," like taking a run? Maybe he's mentioned ways he deals with a hard day at work. Oftentimes just by listening to the stories they tell or watching them with wait staff at restaurants, there can be obvious signs of how they cope with the stresses of life.

Express your emotions in healthy ways:

When he describes a conflict, how does he describe the other person? Is he capable of expressing love and affection for those close to him?

In time does he express appropriate emotions towards you? Emotions expressed either too quickly or not at all can be equally concerning. I don't think any of us are looking for a marriage proposal or professions of undying love on a first date (oh yes, it does happen!), but it is also uncomfortable to be left wondering if he even had a nice time. That doesn't mean he should have to say those exact words. Nonverbal cues are more natural for many men. Did he look you in the eye? Smile? Lean forward and listen attentively? Give you a big hug like maybe he didn't want to let go? These are also very valid forms of expressing how he feels.

Feel positively about life:

When he talks about the future, is he excited about possibilities? When he talks about his day-to-day, is he enjoying experiences? Is every story a problem or a challenge that he doesn't feel can be overcome? How does his overall energy feel to you when you're together?

Self-aware enough to see the areas where you could practice self-improvement but also be able to recognize your strengths:

Now this one is a little trickier early on as, understandably, few people want to talk about any perceived shortcomings on a first date. If someone is actively working on themselves, it shouldn't take too long to see signs of it, though. Also, when they talk about work or conflict, you might see some signs that they are actively taking a look at where they have room for improvement. Conversely, you could see where they could improve but mistakenly believe they are already perfect in every way. Beware of this, as it is a red flag that points to narcissistic tendencies.

A few more areas to pay attention to could be:

Boundaries:
You get the sense that he doesn't have clear boundaries. For example, he tells stories about how his friends and family are always taking up all of his spare time, and people are always demanding favors from him. He always says yes, even if it interferes with other priorities. Conversely, maybe he shows signs of an unwillingness to ever go an inch out of his way for someone or becomes angry at even being asked. These are two extremes of boundary issues, but a man with healthy boundaries is a man who values himself, and you should too.

Emotional availability:
None of this will matter if he's not emotionally available to you. He could be the picture of emotional health, but if none of those emotions are shared with you, then it's not a match. I'm obviously not saying that from the first date, you should know whether he cried when his goldfish died. I'm just saying that if the sharing never gets any deeper than surface level, then it's impossible to grow a deeply connected relationship.

Dating Example: Emotional

Classic Bad Boy

Yes, of course, I've had run-ins with the obligatory bad boys. I wasn't always a dating expert, and even if I had been, I'm only human. I'm bound to make some mistakes along the way.

So the bad boy story that sticks out the most is a guy whom I met when out on the town with my friends.

He was definitely not dull, which is the mass appeal to bad boys. They have their own lives, they don't follow you around like a puppy, and they keep you on your toes. That is the allure, but then comes the bad behavior, which inevitably ends in hurt feelings.

In classic bad-boy fashion, we didn't have very organized dates, but he always had a suggestion of a fantastic place to go. The conversation flowed very easily, and he was always respectful. The problem came whenever I would ask him a question that had to deal with anything emotional in nature.

He would change the topic every single time. He didn't want to discuss anything from what he was like as a kid to how he handled any conflicts with his co-workers at his job.

He was a musician by trade, and he would sometimes talk about conflicts with club owners, entertainment directors, bandmates etc. In those conversations, he would express some serious boundary issues (like saying yes to things he needed to say no to) and then become super defensive when I tried to suggest healthy ways to address the problems.

He would also get furious when he spoke about ex-girlfriends. The fact that he wanted to discuss them at all was strange to me, but I was also a little curious why so I asked. One night I pointed out that he never talked about any of his feelings except anger, and then I asked him if talking about his ex's brought up any other feelings. He abruptly ended the date and then summarily "ghosted" me for two weeks. After one call and one unanswered text, I was officially over it.

I've never suffered from a feeling of scarcity, something I've discovered as the biggest secret in dating, and so he was out of my book. Then one day, I was having a lovely time with my girlfriends, and I got a call from him. They encouraged me to take it just out of curiosity, so I did.

Me: Hello?

Him: Hey, sorry it's been a minute.

Me: It's been weeks. Any particular reason you ghosted me?

Him: Yeah. I don't like all the emotional stuff you're always talking about. It's weird.

Me: Actually, darling, it's not weird at all. It's how people with a healthy grasp of their emotions get to know one another.

Him: Whatever. Well, if you promise not to talk about that stuff anymore, we can give it another try.

Me: I'll have to decline. I'm looking for a man who is comfortable sharing all aspects of his life with me. I genuinely wish you happiness and good fortune. Cheers.

Him: Seriously?

Me: Indeed. Take care now, darling. Goodbye.

I hung up the phone and never looked back.

Key Takeaways from this interaction

1. He showed anger but no healthy coping mechanisms. It is easy to see how this is not conducive to a long-term happy relationship.

2. He showed boundary issues with no solutions. Looking for mutually beneficial solutions to

emotional conflict is essential for healthy connections.

3. His solution, when confronted with emotions, was to run away. Don't bother chasing a man like this, as catching him is never worth the effort.

There was no possibility of a future with a man like that. Healthy relationships require open and honest communication. Can you imagine marrying such a man and having your child come to him with an emotional problem? Nightmare. Even if you don't plan on having children, can you imagine how lonely it would be to grow old with someone that you have no real emotional connection to? That's no way for anyone to live.

Reflection

By knowing yourself, you can see what kind of partner would complement your life well. Are you an optimist by nature? Or are you a recovering pessimist, and overly optimistic people get on your nerves? Does a high level of joyous energy light you up or make you feel tired and want to hide in a quiet room with your favorite book? Are you consistently a very physically loving and close person, or do you need to balance time together with a big dose of alone time? Do you need very clear verbal communication, or are you happy with mostly nonverbal cues? Once you find your own happy place, then it becomes much clearer the type of person that you could build an emotionally satisfying life with.

How this goes on your list:

Let's review the definition of Emotional Wellness... "Emotional Wellness is your ability to cope with life stress, express your emotions in healthy ways and feel positively about life. It includes being self-aware enough to see the areas where you could practice self-improvement but also be able to recognize your strengths. Being emotionally well allows you to communicate your feelings with others and create healthy connections."

Thinking about the areas we've discussed above, what are the positive traits associated with emotional health that need to go on your "Must-haves" list? It's possible that you have also realized some which are an absolute "Deal-breaker," but we're going to save those thoughts for the "Time-saver" section.

You'll see from all the spots available that I deeply believe that this section yields the most beneficial results for long-term happiness!

Potential Social Dimension "Must-Haves":

1.

2.

3.

4.

5.

Brilliant Vixen Secret Bonus #7: Emotional aka Fun Ways to Meet Mr. Right using the Emotional Dimension!

Here's an exercise to help you find activities that bring out your favorite emotions!

Your senses have been shown to be strongly linked to your emotions, so let's think of each of your senses: smell, taste, touch, sight, and sound.
When you think of smell, can you think of an activity that stimulates your sense of smell in an enjoyable way? Perhaps visiting a botanical garden, taking a cooking class, or mixing your own essential oils into a perfume. Your sense of taste could also be stimulated by that same cooking class or by visiting a new restaurant or dessert bar. Touch could be a gardening

class where you stick your hands in fresh soil or something as silly as making a fluffy stuffed animal in one of those shops in the mall. When thinking of sight, the possibilities are endless, an art gallery, hikes in nature, a car show, or a night at the theater! Sound could be anything from a rock concert to a symphony orchestra or even just the sounds of a toad croaking by a pond.

As you are enjoying these activities, either alone or with a friend, take a look around. You should be in an ideal mindset to radiate the kind of energy which will attract positive connections. Or maybe you just use this amazing energy to recharge yourself for your next date?

Extra Bonus

There's an extra secret bonus here that comes from an unlikely place. Therapy! When you consult with a therapist, all kinds of exciting bits come to the surface, including the underlying reasons why you find yourself inexplicably attracted to certain types of men.

Do you have a bad-boy fixation? Therapy!
Only want to date emotionally unavailable men? Therapy!

Run away when a quality man expresses interest in you? Therapy!
The list goes on and on.

Therapy can help you to improve your own happiness and well-being as well as define the man you're looking for with personalized precision. I even recommend bringing your new list in to discuss with your therapist.

"What mental health needs is more sunlight, more candor, and more unashamed conversation." – *Glenn Close*

Let's take better care of ourselves and each other and do away with the antiquated cultural stigma that caring for our mental health is somehow less valid than caring for our physical health!

So with our emotional well-being sorted, let's dive into the last of the 8 dimensions of wellness. The deepest level we can possibly reach.

Chapter Eight

SPIRITUAL

"We are not human beings having a spiritual experience. We are spiritual beings having a human experience." – Pierre Teilhard de Chardin.

L et's define spirituality first for the sake of this book.

"The Spiritual Wellness Dimension is a broad concept that represents one's personal beliefs and values and involves having meaning, purpose, and a sense of balance and peace."
    -SAMHSA

To be clear, this is separate from religion which may or may not be a part of your spirituality. Spirituality is your own personal connection to something bigger than yourself. This personal connection shapes the way you see the world in the most intimate way possible. For that reason, I've saved it for last. We've been peeling back the layers of what makes a perfect match for us, and this is by far the most important one.

The spiritual dimension of wellness defines us in a unique way. This is the innermost definition of who we are at the end of the day. Whether we practice spirituality on solitary nature walks or we attend a house of worship with thousands of other people, the way we view our spirituality is as individual as our fingerprints.

We're going to be reflecting deeply on this final dimension. The answers we find here will provide an undeniable connection when we apply them. For those of you who think about your spirituality on a daily basis, that's incredible. You still might find some new answers about yourself here. For anyone who isn't thinking about their spirituality regularly, then this will be a fascinating look inward.

Let's jump right into it. So what do you believe in? Spend some time here writing what your beliefs are. Subtract any worldly concerns about food, shelter, etc. What is important to you? When you have a moment of stillness in your day, or you take a second to actually watch the sunset, what thoughts are running through your mind? What activities bring a feeling of purpose into your life? What moments fill you with peace? Are there places that have spiritual significance to you? What practices make you feel more connected to the world?

The "Why" game

Everyone's experienced a small child asking "why" repeatedly until they're entirely mentally exhausted. Young children are forming their views of the world, and their innocent questioning is one of the many ways in which they adapt to the world around them. I have a longtime friend who's a professional career counselor, who charges top dollar for her services, and she uses this game with all of her clients. She says, as simple and silly as it might sound when she asks the first two "why's," this game is incredibly powerful. Thanks for the help, Calla. We appreciate you!

We're going to take this innocent questioning and point it at ourselves.

First, let's make a list of 5 things that are deeply important to us.

1.

2.

3.

4.

5.

Now for each of these five items, we're going to the point that child-like curiosity at ourselves and dig four layers deep. Why four, you might ask? Well, anyone can hide for two layers, no problem and then we're just starting to get somewhere by layer three. By layer number four, our politeness has run out, and our honesty is in full gear. If you have one-word answers above, then just start with "Why is _____ important?"

Example: "It's important to be nice to people"

Why is it important to be nice to people?
Because you don't want to hurt their feelings

Why don't you want to hurt their feelings?
Because it's important to treat others well

Why is it important to treat others well?
Because if we can't treat each other like decent
humans, then we've lost.

Why have we lost if we don't treat each other like
decent humans?
Because at the end of the day, all we really have is
each other, and without kindness, the world would be
very bleak.

Now that's getting somewhere! We start with a
surface-level thought and continue to examine it until
we see the underlying reason that it's so important to
us. That's how we truly understand the importance of
it. Completely understanding that importance is the
kind of clarity that's critical to select the person
that's going to be fulfilling to us down to our very
core beliefs. And if you can do that, you'll find
immense satisfaction in your romantic life.

It's important to write down each of these answers to

the question "Why?" because you may be surprised at the direction it goes! It can also be very helpful to review each of your answers later. So after you got out your pen and paper and dug at least 4 layers deep on each one of the points, where did you ultimately end up?

1.

2.

3.

4.

5.

Now we're going to take a look at those 5 answers and try to understand what they have in common or how they work together. All this is to help you answer the one big question.

What brings you purpose in life?

The answer to this question will help you to define, you guessed it, your soulmate!

Dating Example: Spiritual

The NEG

After my one and only date with this gem, I had to take a shower, meditate, burn some sage and more to get the bad vibes off of me.

I met him at a huge party a friend of mine was having. He was funny, really funny. All of his humor was pretty dark, but it all got a chuckle out of me. The first thing he said was something about me breaking my neck wearing my six-inch stilettos. We had some fun banter, and at the end of the night, he asked me out to dinner the following week. I accepted.

The following week, date night rolled around, and we met at a lovely Italian restaurant. He was dressed smartly and welcomed me with a huge smile. We sat down and looked over our menus while we made small talk. After we ordered, then we really started talking. He was just as funny as ever, even making the servers laugh. It was an extremely entertaining date.

I noticed a weird feeling in the pit of my stomach, warning me of some kind of danger. I couldn't put my finger on it just yet. Every time I shared something I thought was cool or interesting, he would make a joke about that too. At first, it started small, like I would mention a movie I enjoyed, and he would say something funny about it. Then I would talk about another restaurant I tried, and he would say something cheeky about it as well. It started to have a strange feeling to it after a while.

Then I decided to test my theory with a subject that would reveal more. I asked him if he'd found a meaningful purpose in his life. Then he really let it rip. Not only did he make fun of the notion of purpose, but he brought it around to "I'm probably one of those chicks who thinks horoscopes are real" For the record, I had made zero horoscope references whatsoever.

He was getting nasty, and his joking was turning mean. His chances at a second date were rapidly evaporating with every word out of his mouth.

Oh, wait a minute, now I get it. To you, everything is stupid. You have to tear down absolutely everything because you're lacking. There's no magic, no mystery, nothing out there bigger than us, just everyone being delusional and stupid for pondering the secrets of life. He was a spiritual void. There were plenty of jokes but, ironically, no joy.

I brought it to his attention that he was actually getting nasty with me, and I had no idea why. He said something about how every woman always plays the victim. I laughed as I got up.

Me: "Ah, some premium misogyny to end the evening. Cheers."
Him: "What, you're leaving?"
Me: "Absolutely"
Him: "What? Why?"
Me: "Because you've forgotten your manners."
Him: "Geez, I was just joking. Come on, sit down."
Me: "I won't, actually. I thought you just joked to keep things fun, but you joke to tear absolutely every-thing down."
Him: "Overreact much? Come on. I didn't realize you were so sensitive."
I sat back down briefly.
Me: "Ok, name one thing in the world that's not absolutely stupid, and I'll stay."
He looked at me like I was on fire.
Me: "That's what I thought. Cheers."

I couldn't get away from him fast enough. I thought back to the first words he said to me back at the party, which were a joking tease, but still negative. Like I said in the beginning, I had to scrub his nega-tive energy off of me. No, thank you, sir. I'll live a life of mystery and magic. You do whatever you like.

Key Takeaways from this interaction

1. If a man is unable to share things that he's passionate about, then it's a red flag. How can anyone have a meaningful purpose in life when they have a complete lack of passion for any subject?

2. A man who jokes about absolutely everything might be using it as a coping mechanism. It's great to joke a lot, and humorous men are a catch but make sure they have the capacity to treat things with reverence if it's important to you.

Reflection:

What does spirituality mean to you? What is the perfect match for you on a spiritual level? These are hard questions, but hopefully, they're a little easier after the "Why?" activity.

What core values are important to you in a man? Once again, perhaps glancing back at the "Why?" activity will give you some ideas.

How this goes on your list:

We're looking to dig beyond the mundane details of life. No matter what changes life throws at you, the purpose that you live it with and the core values that you bring to your day-to-day existence will have a profound effect.

Potential Spiritual Dimension "Must-Haves":
1.

2.

3.

We're looking to dig beyond the mundane details of life. No matter what changes life throws at you, the purpose that you live it with and the core values that you bring to your day-to-day existence will have a profound effect.

Warning: Sometimes people can be very defensive about questions pertaining to the Spiritual dimension, especially if they mistake your meaning for "What religion are you?". If that question is critical for your happiness, then, by all means, ask away, but this is the most profound dimension, so be gentle and lighthearted when asking.

BONUS Player Alert:

If a guy seems bored or irritated by this line of

conversation, then I sincerely doubt he has any long-term aspirations with you. Especially if he changes the topic and wants to return to a surface-level interaction, that's not a good sign.

A quality man would happily dive into a more profound connection in most cases. If a man isn't interested in getting to know you on your deepest levels, then what else could he possibly be there for except sex?

Quality men want much more than just sex; they want someone to be their second half in life. If they aren't happily trying to discover more about you, then they're just not that interested in a meaningful relationship.

Brilliant Vixen Secret Bonus #8: Spiritual aka Fun Ways to Meet Mr. Right using the Spiritual Dimension!

For those of you that are religious, it's pretty easy to see how going to your local temple, church, mosque, shrine, synagogue, or other places of worship would not only be good for your spirituality but also for possibly connecting with a romantic partner on a spiritual level. Many organized religions also have meetups for just this purpose.

For those who aren't necessarily religious, going to places that are intrinsically spiritual or that move you spiritually are incredible places to connect on a deep level.

Take a place like Sedona, Arizona, for example. That place is built on spiritual experiences, from vortex tours to drum circles to crystal shops.

If that's not your brand, then what about relaxing on the beach in the early morning and seeing a man writing in a journal or just admiring the waves?

A yoga class could check multiple boxes at the same time, including the "physical" dimension of wellness along with, well, almost all of the rest of them, to be honest.

Sometimes someone's spiritual connection is just enjoying how amazing it is to be out in nature, so something as simple as a hike could also check multiple boxes!

As this is the last "Secret Bonus," I'm sure you've noticed a theme. Do things you love, try things you might love, and generally, just search out ways to enjoy life more fully! While enjoying your particular brand of an ideal life, you are much more likely to run across someone you would enjoy spending that ideal life with. Please consider sticking with the activities that you enjoy the most. Familiarity quite often makes it easier to strike up a conversation with someone new. Also, have you ever noticed that people who live their life in a genuinely connected and joyful way are intrinsically more attractive?

Chapter Nine

"TIME SAVERS" AKA "DEAL BREAKERS"

"Time is the most valuable asset you don't own. You may or may not realize it yet, but how you use or don't use your time is going to be the best indication of where your future is going to take you."
    -Marc Cuban (Patel, 2018)

I saved this last portion of any list for the very end. You've spent a ton of time digging deep and creating all kinds of possibilities for a fantastic new list that includes all the wonderful things that you truly value in a partner. I applaud you for that! I saved this until the end because I wanted to make sure that all my Brilliant Vixens would approach it when they're in a completely open and balanced mental, emotional, and spiritual state.

Knowing as early as possible that someone is not for you is extremely important because you don't want to spend any more time and energy than necessary on something that is destined to fail. Taking just a little time now can save you some pain and heartache later by helping you avoid investing in the wrong connections.

As such, this chapter is here to help you learn more about "Time-savers" so that, hopefully, you can spot them in the beginning phase of getting to know each other. This may even help you avoid some bad first dates altogether!

Everyone is different, so do not expect me to give you a list of steady, unbreakable rules when it comes to "Deal-breakers," aka "Time-savers." Rather than that, I'm here to help and encourage you to find your own unbreakable boundaries, your own uncrossable lines and your own strong standards.

Without further ado, let's dive deeper into this topic and uncover the essence of time-savers!

Why You Need Your Time-Savers

This is something that most people don't have at the forefront of their minds when dating, but few things are more important than time. There's never truly enough of it, it's not something you can take back, and it most certainly is not something you can just order more of with your credit card.

As I mentioned in the beginning, your time is limited and precious, dear Brilliant Vixen. You literally do not have any time to waste on men who are not what you need, want or are looking for. Wouldn't you rather use all that time either searching for someone worthy of you or just working on yourself, growing, and feeling good about who you are now?

That is precisely why I prefer to use the term "time-savers" rather than "deal-breakers." The first one emphasizes the essence of what is truly important for a Brilliant Vixen, while the latter has a certain negative connotation to it that is just not befitting of the positive outlook on life I continuously promote.

A "time-saver" is, in essence, a term to use when someone shows behaviors that are so unacceptable to you that you can move on and not waste a moment more on them. When someone says something is a "deal-breaker," there are at least two parties that need to come to an agreement. It implies that there was a deal in place, and now you must come to an agreement to break it. When I use "time-saver," however, this puts all the power of choice in your hands.

You can look at the behavior and decide that you are grateful they have shown their true colors to you sooner rather than later, and therefore you are free to happily move on with your life, searching for someone who is a better fit for you. Because remember, scarcity is an invention, and there are plenty of other options out there, right?

A "deal-breaker" can feel like a small end-of-the-world scenario when you really like a man. That might make you feel more inclined to break your own rules to accommodate that man into your life despite him showing unbecoming behaviors which clearly aren't conducive to long-term happiness.

Therefore, from here on in this chapter, I will use "time-savers" every time I refer to things men do that should not be acceptable to a Brilliant Vixen. I do want to emphasize that I am not trying to set your rules for your life. I just want to speak to you about some behaviors you should at least consider as unacceptable. You can add your own time-savers to this list, and you can delete or change those you might not entirely agree with.

Time-savers are all about not beating yourself up over things you can't change (because remember, you can't really change someone else, you can only change your attitude towards them).

Time-savers are about accepting things as they are and moving on to find your own happiness.

Because, my lovelies, your happiness is out there, waiting for you. So don't waste your time on someone who is just not "the one" for you.

Absolute Time-Savers You Should Consider

Now that we've defined "time-savers," we know why they're so critical to our success in dating. An important thing to keep in mind is that a Brilliant Vixen sets her own rules — and that's exactly what I encourage you to do as well. This section will help to give you some guidelines that should be on every woman's list.

The following are some behaviors you should definitely consider as unacceptable. As mentioned before, feel free to add your own list of things that don't work for you. They might seem trivial to someone else, but chances are that, if you are already thinking of them, you should probably not accept them in a man. It's one thing to be flexible; it's an entirely different thing to accept something that upsets you or goes against your beliefs and principles.

That being cleared up, here are some behaviors that should be universally considered unworthy of a true Brilliant Vixen:

Lying

You cannot build a lasting relationship on a foundation of lies because you cannot build a real life together when you don't know what his reality is. This may sound extreme, but if you catch a man in small lies, then chances are that there are bigger lies yet to come.

Can you think of a time when a man lied to you, and that red flag was a harbinger of heartbreak to come? The worst one that I can think of is actually from my sister. She was dating a man who was from out of town but visited Las Vegas (where we live) very regularly.

Pretty early on, she saw his ID and realized that he had lied about his age. He said he was younger than he was. She excused it, saying he looked younger than he was, and she thought it was cute that he thought a few years would discourage her from dating him. I saw it as a red flag. I then started to connect a few dots and wonder if he might already be romantically attached back home. My sister said he was almost always available when she called and that he would never do that to her. After all, he was in town almost every week. How could he do that alone if he had a wife or girlfriend?

He treated her well, taking her to romantic dinners and spoiling her with gifts. He spent almost every minute of his time in town with her right by his side. Still, something felt off to me. Several months later, he convinced her to move hundreds of miles away to the coast of CA, and he set her up in a cute little apartment. I told her that big sis wasn't driving all that way to come get her when things fell apart, as I'd already told her I didn't trust him.

Of course, barely more than a month had passed, and I was in a truck filled with all her belongings while driving my crying little sis back to Las Vegas. She told me all the lies she had uncovered bit by bit while far from home and missing her friends and family.

She found out that he had been coming to Vegas not just to visit her but because he was dealing drugs. She also learned that he was married. He had no intention of leaving his wife, and he thought that if she was alone in his city that she would be so dependent on him that she would just accept that.

There were many other smaller lies that surrounded these devastating new facts. Including the one she didn't initially tell me about, which should definitely have been her "time-saver." When she saw his ID, she also realized that he was using his middle name as his first name. Now alone, this isn't a problem, especially if the person tells you. Some people consider fudging your age by a few years to be a "white lie" that also isn't a problem. But together, I believe a pattern was emerging.

At what point in this story would you have left? Would it have been at the very first sign? Or would you still be living in that lonely little apartment, just waiting for the day when he might leave his wife because you're such an amazing woman? (You are amazing, by the way, but sadly that has very little bearing in situations like these!)

This story leads very easily into the next time-saver...

Cheating

If a man cheats, that isn't something that is going to improve, no matter how special you are. This is a definite character flaw that the man will have to work on if he wants to have a quality relationship. But let's not let him work through this on your time while causing you heartache.

Please also keep in mind that if he's willing to cheat on someone else with you, then it's only a matter of time until he's willing to cheat on you with someone else. This is about who he is more than it's about who you are.

There are actually some very interesting studies out there about cheating, technically referred to as "extradyadic sex". Some of the reasons people step out on their significant others are not what I thought they would be at all.

I found this fascinating study posted on Dr. Scott Stanley's blog. Dr. Stanley is a noteworthy research professor who conducts studies on marriage and romantic relationships.

"Unmarried Cheating: Stepping Out in Unmarried, Serious Romantic Relationships"

"What I will now list are the variables (in no particular order) that we found to be associated with having extradyadic sex over the period of time studied (1.5 yrs).

Individual variables associated with extradyadic sex

- Having more sexual partners prior to the present relationship
  - Greater use of alcohol
  - Having parents who never married

Individual variables NOT associated with extradyadic sex

- Gender (males were not more likely than females to cheat)
  - Age
  - Education
  - Religiousness

- Having children (with partner or from prior relationships)

- Parental divorce

Relationship variables associated with extradyadic sex

- Lower relationship satisfaction

- Lower levels of dedication (commitment) to the partner

- Higher levels of negative communication

- A history of physical aggression in the relationship

- Not having mutual plans for marriage

- Suspicion of partner having sex with other(s)

- Partner has had sex with another

Relationship variables NOT associated with extradyadic sex

- Frequency of sex in present relationship

- Satisfaction with sex in present relationship

- Living together"

http://slidingvsdeciding.blogspot.-com/2013/07/unmarried-cheating-stepping-out-in.html

I don't know about you, but this was really eye-opening.

This section really blew me away.

"Individual variables NOT associated with extradyadic sex"

"- Gender (males were not more likely than females to cheat)"
Wow, no difference!

"- Age"
Definitely not something people grow out of with age.

"- Education"
You can be book smart and still not be smart enough to not throw away a good thing.

"- Religiousness"
This was really surprising. Even people who believe on a deep spiritual level that what they're doing could have much larger negative implications have no bearing. There was no statistical difference between religious people and non-religious people.

"- Having children (with partner or from prior relationships)"
Family stability doesn't really enter into the equation.

"- Parental divorce"
I thought that this would make a difference in a person's mind about family stability, but apparently not.

Cheating is not only emotionally devastating, which is reason enough to avoid these types at all costs. But every time someone cheats on you, they're introducing a serious health risk to you. If a guy is sleeping with someone else, just like we learned back in health class, now this new person's whole sexual history is automatically linked to your current health. Some sexually transmitted diseases have permanent health implications, and others are even life-threatening.

I know this isn't new information, but I bring it up to put it into context.

A man who cheats on you cares so little for you that he would be willing to risk your health just to have a sexual conquest.

That is not a man who's worth having around for any reason. Even if he used a condom, condoms break.

They work very well but not a perfect 100%, so health risks are never completely mitigated.

Equally important is that they clearly can't be trusted. They're lying to you in the most hurtful way possible. In the rare case of a polyamorous or open relationship, boundaries are generally still set, and if he breaks those boundaries, all the same principles apply.

I personally can't fathom a reason to tolerate this behavior, but ultimately the choice is yours. Let's just say I highly recommend this being on your absolute "Time-savers" list.

Emotionally Unavailable/Low Commitment

These types of men can have intrigue to them because they're not actively chasing women the way most men do. This can sometimes read as confidence or mystique. But it's not for a healthy reason.

For men like this, they're not letting you in for a reason, and that reason usually falls into three common but equally undateable categories.

1. They're just looking for sex and don't want to get to know you.

2. They're incapable of letting anyone in emotionally.

3. They're just not that into you.

These types of men are not willing/able to have any kind of true bond with you. Without a bond between the two of you it's not possible to have a meaningful relationship.

This type of man is the definition of being with someone yet still alone.

Being in a relationship with an emotionally unavailable man is like being trapped on a desert island and dying of thirst. You're surrounded by an ocean of water that won't nourish you.

For that reason, I highly recommend that you put this on your absolute "Time-savers" list.

Anger/Violence

This one is not only scary, but it can also be an extremely serious risk to your health. A man who displays these traits can be someone who can make your life a living Hell. Someone with anger problems can cause trouble in every single area of your life, so be on the lookout for early signs that they have these issues.

Early warning signs can include, but are definitely not limited to:

Being rude to wait-staff
Road Rage
Becoming overly upset by common text messages and calls
Getting visibly frustrated by not finding a parking space
Having several strong negative opinions on one date
Extreme sarcasm
Treating people like they're stupid
Acting as though they're above others
Having to calm themselves down on a date or making excuses for their anger. "Sorry, I got worked up. It's just..."
Aggressive behavior with other males (sticking their chest out, talking tough, inventing problems with other men, trying to intimidate other men, etc.)

This anger can lead to several kinds of mistreatment, including verbal, emotional, psychological, or, as I stated earlier, even physical abuse.

So if you're seeing signs of anger/violence, please do not ignore them. This is a big one. I highly recommend that you add this to your absolute "Timesavers" list.

Your Personal Time Savers

Now that we've reviewed some fairly universal timesavers, let's return to thinking about some that are more personal. Everyone should have their own timesavers that are built on the core principles of that person. By that, I mean who you are at the deepest part of yourself.

Here are a few common individual time savers:

Do you have a child? What behaviors are completely unacceptable around your kid?
Are you deeply rooted in a belief system? Do they have to believe the same thing or at least respect it?
Are you strongly rooted in your political beliefs? Are you open to them not sharing those beliefs?

The Final Test

Ok, so you're getting ready to write down these timesavers. There's one final step before we get to the action.

Imagine that by the stars aligning perfectly that you end up on a date with your favorite celebrity crush. They're head over heels smitten with you, and they can't wait to whisk you away on a romantic whirlwind romance.

You just had your first amazing kiss, and you're wrapping up dinner. You're about to jet-set away to paradise together. Then they let slip one of the dreaded deal-breakers you're thinking about putting on your list.

If it's bad enough for you to call off your fairytale date with this stunning celebrity, then it has earned its place on your list. If not, it has to go. That's a fun way to keep your time-savers honest. That's the final test.

If you decide that there wouldn't be even one thing on your time-savers list under these circumstances, then one of three things is true...

1. Your time-savers haven't been thought about in a serious enough way. ie They aren't deeply important enough to you.

2. You need to seriously consider whether you have an issue with maintaining healthy boundaries.

3. Your crush on this celebrity is simply so out of control that all reason has gone out the window. Girl, it happens to the best of us but let's make sure it doesn't train-wreck our lives, ok?

So list down your time-savers and watch out for the signs. Be crystal clear about leaving bad news guys behind when you do. Close the door behind, and never look back.

You are worthy of SO much more than all that garbage!

So when filling out our list, please consider using these universal time-savers. We want to avoid loading up a bizarre list of reasons to eliminate people for relatively minor infractions, so make sure to keep your time-savers genuine. Each one of your reasons has to be something that there is absolutely no way around for you.

With that in mind, let's make a list of the top 5 traits that you will absolutely no longer accept, no matter who it is!

Time-savers

1.

2.

3.

4.

5.

Now take just a second to compare them to the deal breakers you put at the beginning of the book. Reflect on any changes and see how you feel about them. If none of them have changed, you're either 100% on the right track already, or you need to give it just one more shot.

Chapter Ten

BONUS CHAPTER DATING LIST CLICHÉS THAT STEAL WOMEN'S HAPPINESS

I n the pursuit of finding Mr. Right, some women put things on their lists that end up making them miserable.

These unfortunate low-vibrational trappings of modern society insidiously creep into our subconscious, thanks to the media at large.

It's important to review these, even if you know they don't apply to you, for two reasons.

1. They can give insight into how you're looking at other dimensions to make sure you're steering clear of decisions for your list which won't actually add to your happiness.

2. You will have all the information you need at hand to help others. Especially any friends you see heading down an unhelpful path.

There are many different ways in which a proper love list takes a wrong turn, but these are the four most notorious happiness saboteurs of all time.

Six-pack abs

If this isn't on your list, then you can either skip this section or use it to deconstruct how you are thinking about any of the other Physical based items on your list.

If you are currently rocking 6 pack abs and enjoy the level of hard work and dedication it consistently takes for most adults to achieve them, then yes, you have earned the right to put this on your list! It is healthy to want to be with someone who values the same things as we do at the level that we do.

If not, then take a deep breath because this next section is for you. Try not to forget that I love you and only want to see you happy!

Oh, my lovelies, this one does tend to throw so many brilliant women off the deep end, doesn't it? Six-pack abs are nice to look at, but that's it. More so, six-pack abs require extreme dedication and a strict lifestyle to support them. Why does that matter? He's the one doing the crunches, not me, right? Technically yes, but as with most things, there's much more to it than that.

Throughout this entire book, we're looking for balance. We're finding the ideal balance between what you think you want and what's actually going to make you happy.

For example, here, if you say you want a guy with 10 percent body fat who's a UFC fighter, then if you got exactly that, what would life look like?

My husband, Liam, has worked with professional athletes, mostly fighters, for a living. So I've gotten to know what their lives look like. Up early working out, more working out, eating, being cranky at particular times before the competition, not being able to have indulgent food around them, and extra support of all kinds during training camp.

Liam has told me that the ladies around them that don't subscribe to that lifestyle never become their girlfriends. They stay in the "fun only" department.

The point is that they're so busy on their trajectory that there's no way they can take someone seriously that doesn't mirror that lifestyle with them to at least some degree. Their whole day is being surrounded by beautiful women who exercise rigorously as part of their daily routine. By default, they're surrounded by ring girls and other professional athletes. If a woman looks out of place in that world, she will feel it sooner rather than later.

"Well, some professional athletes have pretty wives that don't have anything to do with their sport. I'll just do that." This is a desperate argument that I've heard from some lovely ladies who were trying to find an easy mode to date athletes. The problem with it is that you don't see the behind-the-scenes home life. The wives of professional athletes are very involved in the well-being of their husbands. Just because they're wearing designer clothing in the VIP skybox doesn't mean that they're not incredibly supportive and knowledgeable about what their husbands need. The ones who aren't involved with their husbands' lives don't retire with them, to put it lightly.

Men with six-pack abs are also rare worldwide. The percentage of men on television, on social media and in magazines and so on sporting impressive visible abs is not telling of the world at large.

"If we add up the percentage of people that are actively training in the world (who probably don't all have visible abs) with the fact that only 5% of the world population has a body fat percentage of less than 13%, which is when abs start to become visible, we can conclude that 1% of the world population (or even less) has visible abs." -Eliass AL

If you previously had this on your list, I would take a moment to seriously consider whether it really belongs on a "Must-haves" list or if it's really more suited to a "hey, that would be nice" list. That's not the kind of list we're making here!

But first, let's tackle another one of the most notorious physical traits in list history.

6 Feet Tall

This has got to be the most prolific saboteur of women's lists in history. Most notably, the illusive man over 6 foot (1.82 m) rule. I cannot tell you how many incredible women automatically reject amazing men just because they're not 6 feet tall or over.

I'm doing this as a public service to all my lovelies out there who have let a frankly silly number sabotage their pursuit of happiness. For starters, let's look at the statistical data for men over 6 feet tall worldwide, shall we?

The number of men who are over 6 feet tall in the entire world is only 12%. This does not even begin to cross-reference two other essential factors.

15% of men in the United States are over 6 feet tall, which is 3% higher than the worldwide average. Of those men, 3.6 percent of men in the United States identify as gay. So the number of straight males over 6 feet tall in the United States is arguably around 12.4% in the worst-case scenario.

As of 2020, 64% of people in the world are married. So that further reduces the overall dating options when seeking men over 6 feet tall. This brings our tally to 6%, at best.

Women who prefer to date single, heterosexual men who are also over 6 feet tall have statistically reduced their chances of happiness to 6% or less worldwide.

If we look at the average height of men worldwide, they're not even close to 6 feet.

"The average height of men in the world is about 171 cm or 5'6 and a half, though this isn't an exact figure due to obvious reasons but this does sum up the average height of men around the world to some extent."- *https://colonelheight.com/percentage-of-world-population-over-6-feet-tall/*

So now that we've seen statistical evidence that finding an available man over 6 feet tall who enjoys the company of women is unlikely, let's look at some desirable men under 6 feet tall for fun.

After a bit of research and a peek at more than a few lists like "Sexiest Men Alive" I've compiled a quick list of 24 male celebrities, from actors to musicians, who all have one thing in common. All the men on this list are under 5'10". So not only are these men not the arbitrary 6-foot-tall marker, but they're not even close. It would be a reasonable assumption that these gentlemen aren't struggling to find romantic partners. So if you're setting a filter on a dating profile to over 6 feet, then all of these men would automatically be discarded as possibilities.

Male Celebrities under 5'10 (in alphabetical order by first name)

Bruno Mars 5'5" (1.65M)
Daniel Radcliffe — 5'5" (1.65 m)
Dave Franco - 5'7" (1.7 M)
Ed Sheeran, - 5'8" (1.73 m)
Elijah Wood, 5'6" (1.67 m)
Mark Wahlberg, 5'8" (1.73 meters)
Robert Downey Jr., — 5'8½" (1.74 m)
James McAvoy, 5'7" (1.7 M)
Jared Leto, — 5'9" (1.75 m)
Jeremy Renner, — 5'9" (1.75 m)
Joe Jonas, - 5'7" (1.7 M)
Johnny Depp, 5'9" (1.75 m)
Josh Hutcherson, 5'5" (1.65 m)
Kanye West, 5'8" (1.73 m)
Kit Harington, — 5'8" (1.73 m)
Lil Wayne, - 5'5" (1.65 m)
Nick Jonas, - 5'6" (1.67 m)
Olly Murs, 5'9" (1.75 m)
Pete Wentz, - 5'7" (1.7 M)
Taylor Lautner, 5'8½" (1.74 m)
Tom Cruise, - 5'7" (1.7 M)
Tom Holland, 5'8" (1.73 m)

Usher, 5'7" (1.7 M)
Zac Efron, 5'8" (1.73 m)

So to the ladies suffering from this terrible 6-foot affliction, to be clear, you would turn down a date from every single guy on this list? I have my doubts that anyone reading this wouldn't even entertain the idea of a date with at least one of them.

Now that we've seen some great examples of desirable men under 6 feet, what are the chances that your Prince Charming is also less than 6 feet tall? Statistically speaking, it's incredibly likely.

Now a more suitable adjustment can be to look for men who are taller than us if height happens to be important to you. Having to look slightly up at a man is attractive to many women, including me. I myself am only 5'2½", so every man on that list is one I would literally be looking up at. This applies to women who feel more comfortable having men be physically larger than them. There are also so many men that are the same height as many women, which visually makes us symmetrical and, therefore, visually balanced.

Wanting a guy who's taller than you is fine if it makes you feel more feminine or has some other deeply seated reason for you but assigning an arbitrary number like 6 feet tall is an unnatural metric for attraction. Not to mention statistically unlikely. Six feet tall men have no guarantees other than which shelf in the cupboard they can reach without a step ladder. This is not a metric that can have any real bearing on your happiness as a romantically fulfilled woman.

So let's agree to do away with the 6 feet rule for our collective happiness. I will not condone letting a silly number diminish your chances of finding true love, just as I would not tolerate a man basing a woman's worth on her dress size or, just as horrifying, her bra size.

Prestigious Career

Many of the women I interview and ask what they're looking for in a potential partner have mentioned something along the lines of "A doctor, a Firefighter, or oooh, I love a man in uniform!"

I always ask why? For example, why a doctor?

Are you worried about your health? Regular checkups

are probably a healthier way to take care of that than centering your love life around it.

Are you worried about financial stability? Many professions make enough to be financially comfortable, especially if you're contributing to the household income.

Are you thinking about how good it would look to friends and family? If they wouldn't be happy that you found a healthy and happy match regardless of his profession, then their outlook is flawed and not in your best interest.

Perhaps you've listed "Doctor," but the trait you truly value is "Well Educated," or "Well Respected," or "Capable of caring for others"?

One of the only healthy reasons that I have heard for a very specific career carrying any weight at all in a romantic relationship is that you are also in that career. This applies only if it happens to be a difficult career to understand the hours, work culture or responsibilities unless you're also in it.

If you have a very specific career listed in your "Must-Haves," then please take a moment and think about the possibility that what you actually value could be something deeper than just a job title.

Six-Figures...

We've already touched on three of the worst saboteurs of women's happiness, which are that a man needs to be over 6 feet tall, have six-pack abs and have one of a select few careers. Now for the fourth serving of unhappiness, the infamous six-figure salary.

"In full-year 2020 – the most-recent full-year earn-ings for 2021 – the cutoffs for the top percentiles were as follows (for all workers):"- PK

Sex: Male

Top 10%

$151,425.00

Top 5%

$206,691.00

Top 1%

$428,500.00

-PK, https://dqydj.com/income-by-sex/

The highest number in any given sampling maxed out at 23% of men earning a six-figure salary in 2021. As we did with height, let's also look at the statistics of that best-case scenario number.

162 million men in the United States
-77% of men who make under six figures (Best recorded number)

-64% of people in the world are married
-3.6% of men in the United States identify as homosexual
7.45% of men in the United States earn six figures, are heterosexual and are unmarried, according to the most generous studies.

That is based on the best numbers I could find. Most studies find the number to be closer to 10% of men earning six figures as the starting point, which looks like this.

162 million men in the United States
-90% of men who make under six figures (average studies)
-64% of people in the world are married
-3.6% of men in the United States identify as homosexual

3.26% of men in the United States earn six figures, are heterosexual and are unmarried, according to most studies.

Ok, statistics class is over for now. This one requirement has crept onto a shockingly growing number of women's lists, and it needs to be addressed. Women who make this a hard requirement for dating have already put themselves at an overwhelming disadvantage. With this requirement alone, you've already increased your competition to the top 10% of women in the world. If you add any more requirements like height, for example, then you're strictly competing with the top 1% of women in the world, which means your competition is comprised of celebrities and centerfolds.

If that's still important to you, then you need to be willing to put in the work in all parts of your life to become competitive with the 1% of women. If that is your chosen path, then you have my best wishes, and I genuinely hope for your success.

As a steadfast supporter of my lovely ladies around the globe, I do not judge women for the lives that appeal to them. What I do is hold them accountable for those decisions. I encourage them to simply make a different choice if they find that the way they're doing things is no longer in alignment with their purpose.

How you look at the financial wellness dimension will determine how romance and money intersect for you personally. Making sure someone is relatively financially stable if you're looking to be with them long-term is not only reasonable, it's putting the focus on the long-term survivability of your budding romance. That being said, what's unhealthy is having an inequitable mindset.

How does that relate to money? Well, here it is. If you want to be 100% financially supported by a man in a relationship, it's imperative to ask yourself what you will bring to the relationship. This is frequently asked:

"So, what do you bring to the table?"

"I am the table" is a disturbing response that is growing rapidly, particularly the younger in age you go. I implore you to encourage women whom you hear applying this type of logic to give it a second thought. What they aren't understanding is that the relationship itself is the "table" in this metaphor. I'm giving these women the benefit of the doubt that they don't actually believe that they are "the relationship" in its entirety. So if I'm mistaken and a growing number of women genuinely think that just being present is contribution enough to any given relationship, then they're not exhibiting the traits of a high-value woman. It shows a complete lack of teamwork and a total disinterest in making a meaningful contribution to the two of you as a couple. If a man were to sit down and say, "I'm handsome, provide for me financially, and I plan on giving nothing back," that would sound ridiculous, wouldn't it? So enough of that particular type of silliness, then. Agreed?

We can't have ladies banking on a man to only admire their physical beauty until the end of time with no other elements to the relationship. That plan is ripe for failure over time. There are new beautiful young women arriving in their 20s every single day. Statistically speaking, when asking single men of all ages what the preferred age of a woman would be for romantic reasons, the universal answer arrived firmly at women in their 20s being the most attractive across the board.

"Dataclysm" author and OkCupid co-founder Christian Rudder uses numbers from the dating site to show how women and men differ in the ages of the people they're attracted to. Men, regardless of their age, tend to say women in their early 20s look best, while women are most attracted to men their own age." -Pamela Engle https://www.businessinsider.com/author/pamela-engel.

So in order to consider your relationship secure, a man would have to value not only access to your physical beauty but all of the uniquely wonderful bits that make your relationship something he cherishes. You want a man to fall in love with you as a whole. You want this to be a love that celebrates the depth and richness of both of you combined. Besides, if it's only physical beauty a woman offers, then she's staying at the most superficial level.

Superficial levels of connection only offer superficial levels of loyalty.

Beautiful relationships are built on mutual love and respect. Part of that is to contribute to the relationship in some way. When you contribute to the relationship, the man feels appreciated, and that appreciation is part of a long-lasting romance. That contribution can take a number of forms, and no two relationships are the same.

And now, returning to the light.

Thank you for your attention during that trip through the four most notorious saboteurs of women's happiness. As I've heard these so many times, I felt like I would be doing my readers a disservice if I didn't cover them when writing this book.

The intention with this bonus chapter was to make sure that there are no hidden happiness thieves on women's lists, making it hard for them to see Mr. Right.

Next, we'll move on to a review of all your potential list items and finalize this new version of your "Must-Haves" and Time-Savers"!

Chapter Eleven

CONCLUSION: THE REAL LIST, "MUST-HAVES" AND "TIME-SAVERS" THAT LEAD TO AMAZING RELATIONSHIPS!

"Our goals can only be reached through a vehicle of a plan, in which we must fervently believe, and upon which we must vigorously act. There is no other route to success." – Pablo Picasso.

During this process, with each chapter, you've written down possibilities for your new list with ideas based on solid psychological studies.

First, let's take a look back at your old list from the beginning. It's way back there in the beginning "Preface" section. I'm guessing that it's pretty far from what would actually provide you with what you're really looking for in life. Now let's finalize the new version of your list that will help guide you toward happiness. That's what I'm here for, to help you make every part of your dating life brilliant!

Let's take a look at all the possibilities you've written down for your new list, shall we? As you copy them into this new section, let's take another look at them and go ahead and leave behind anything that just doesn't seem that important anymore. Please choose at least one to write down from each section though. We're trying to create a balanced life and a balanced list!

Chapter 1
Potential Physical Dimension "Must-Haves":
1.

2.

3.

Chapter 2
Potential Occupational Dimension "Must-Haves":
1.

2.

3.

Chapter 3
Potential Financial Dimension "Must-Haves":
1.

2.

3.

Chapter 4
Potential Environmental Dimension "Must-Haves":
1.

2.

3.

Chapter 5
Potential Intellectual Dimension "Must-Haves":
1.

2.

3.

Chapter 6
Potential Social Dimension "Must-Haves":

1.

2.

3.

Chapter 7
Potential Emotional Dimension "Must-Haves":

1.
2.
3.
4.
5.

Chapter 8
Potential Spiritual Dimension "Must-Haves":

1.

2.

3.

I would actually like you to work backward and
choose at least one but possibly more than one trait
from each dimension. Just circle them on your lists
for now. Now count them. Do you have more than

10? Take another look at the circled traits and decide which ones to let go of. If you have less than 10 but at least one from each dimension then that's ok too!

Now, take a look at the traits on your lists that you didn't circle. If a man was every single one of the things on your list but none of those would you be happy? Think about why if not. Is something you didn't circle actually more important or are you just having a hard time letting go of something that's inconsequential and merely surface-level?

 *Here's an example that has jammed up a few of my lovelies... you know I don't subscribe to surface-level specifics like "6 feet". I do, however, believe it's important to be attracted to your romantic partner. So don't feel bad if you have "great chemistry" or the like on your list. This is a romantic partner, not just a best friend, that you are looking for after all.

So after review do you have your 10? Go ahead and write them below on your new and improved list!

*Don't worry if you go on a few dates and then feel the need to review and revise your list. It's a sign of growth, not a mistake.

Ten things you want in a man
aka "Must-Haves"

1.
2.
3.
4.
5.
6.
7.
8.
9.
10.

You already have your "Time-Savers" at the end of
Chapter 9 so copy them down below.

5 things you absolutely won't tolerate in a romantic
partner
aka "Deal-Breakers" or "Time-Savers"

1.
2.
3.
4.
5.

So what's left to do now? I say celebrate! Do a little dance, have your favorite beverage, call a friend and share! But also there's just a few juicy bits left so... finish the book!

A word of caution: dates should not be looked at as job interviews.

This has been a recurring theme for many comedy bits, and there is a grain of truth to it, but the error is to adopt an interview mindset during the date. You're both looking at each other and assessing your level of compatibility (quality men are assessing much more than your level of attractiveness and willingness to sleep with them).

This doesn't mean that during the course of the conversation you won't ask questions or find answers about whether he's compatible with the "Must-Haves" or whether one of those "Time-Savers" is going to do just that.

As I've stated earlier, a man who is not interested in talking about the important things in life seems suspicious. No matter what the personality type is, all men deal with these 8 Dimensions of Wellness in their daily lives. They likely won't label them as such but that doesn't change that fact. Even though you may be keeping them in mind, try to stay in the moment and just enjoy a curious conversation. A date should never feel like a one-sided interview!

AFTERWORD

"If one does not know to which port one is sailing, no wind is favorable." -Lucius Annaeus Seneca

---

I created this book to help all of the lovely ladies I encounter who are simply looking for the wrong thing, which they're sure to find. As the quote above states, if you don't know where you're going, nothing is going to help you. This book is here to help you plot the map to what you're looking for.

So let your new list be your map to Mr. Right, and enjoy the journey of finding him. There's another bonus in this book that you can download for free. It's a gratitude journal that will help you destress and appreciate life as it is while you work on making it even better!

I hope you've enjoyed the process of looking at your own 8 Dimensions of Wellness as you define your ideal partner. These dimensions are such a powerful base for us to check in with. If we're in a place where we're happy with each of our 8 Dimensions, then by default, our lives should feel balanced and abundant. I've really enjoyed using these as check-in points with my friends and family as well.

I'd like to thank Dr. Peggy Swarbrick publicly. These 8 Dimensions of Wellness are a fantastic basis for us to build an effective list on. With this new list, we can leave no stone unturned in our pursuit of happiness with a fantastic high-quality man who's interested in a long-term romance.

Before I go, I'd like to thank each and every one of you for your kind attention. Your support means the world to me, and I wouldn't be a professional writer without you. Cheers, my treasured vixens!

With much love,

Victoria Knightley

Free Gift For My Readers!

A Relaxing Gratitude Journal to unwind while you find Mr. Right

90 Days of Positivity and Fun

Free additional printable pages for your gratitude practice!

SOURCES

Al, Eliass. "What Percentage of Men Have Abs?" *Ectomorphing*, 2 July 2022, ectomorphing.com/what-percentage-of-men-have-abs/. Accessed 10 Nov. 2022.

"Albert Einstein Quote: "Creativity Is Intelligence Having Fun."" *Quotefancy.com*, quotefancy.com/quote/1578/Albert-Einstein-Creativity-is-intelligence-having-fun. Accessed 10 Nov. 2022.

"BrainyQuote." *BrainyQuote*, BrainyQuote, 2019, www.brainyquote.com/quotes/albert_einstein_174001. Accessed 10 Nov. 2022.

Caputo, Yvonne. "Wellness: What Is It Really and What Works?" *Saint Lukes/ Penn Foundation*, www.pennfoundation.org/news-events/articles-of-interest/wellness-what-is-it-really-and-what-works/. Accessed 9 Nov. 2022.

"Deepak Chopra Quote: "a Job Is How You Make Money. A Career Is How You Make Your Mark. A Calling Is How You Acknowledge a Higher Vision, Whate..."" *Quotefancy.com*, quotefancy.com/quote/792773/Deepak-Chopra-A-job-is-how-you-make-money-A-career-is-how-you-make-your-mark-A-calling-is. Accessed 9 Nov. 2022.

Delagran, Louise. "How Does Your Personal Environment Impact Your Wellbeing?" *Taking Charge of Your Health & Wellbeing*, University of Minnesota, www.takingcharge.csh.umn.edu/how-does-your-personal-environment-impact-your-wellbeing. Accessed 10 Nov. 2022.

Dew, Jeffrey, et al. "Examining the Relationship between Financial Issues and Divorce." *Wiley Online Library*, 12 Sept. 2012, onlinelibrary.wiley.com/doi/epdf/10.1111/j.1741-3729.2012.00715.x?referrer_access_token=grwZYnQSLhCIcZf1nly274ta6bR2k8j-HoKrdpFOxC666fuC-uLoz6F9mISEPjugzuuEM4ul-CIwC_8DQNjj6gLeAX6GffLInfTza13O_1gBnv_oFxYeXCD-

k3ya1NHqyyM3UJL_KVSX_ezMTZ-lLIh_RT1rYwZNaPnr-
EmdmdKvUAoeujCBj2CHfhVYGmCsKD-
7EkDWK6BqKDL88KjAH_cJ_FjbNxAX0EntDbdctkK-
to42Cfe8TmIDucQVbuustvIm. Accessed 10 Nov. 2022.

Diener, Ed, et al. *Social Well-Being: Research and Policy Recommen-dations*.

Engel, Pamela. "CHARTS: Guys like Women in Their Early 20s regardless of How Old They Get." *Business Insider*, 21 Oct. 2014, www.businessinsider.com/dataclysm-shows-men-are-attracted-to-women-in-their-20s-2014-10.

FOGEL, SYDNEY. "These Are the Shortest Men in Holly-wood." *Livingly*, www.livingly.com/These+Are+The+Short-est+Men+In+Hollywood. Accessed 10 Nov. 2022.

Gates, Gary J. "How Many People Are Lesbian, Gay, Bisexual, and Transgender?" *Williams Institute*, Apr. 2011, williamsinsti-tute.law.ucla.edu/publications/how-many-people-lgbt/. Accessed 9 Nov. 2022.

GoodTherapy.org. "The 8 Dimensions of Wellness: Where Do You Fit In?" *GoodTherapy.org Therapy Blog*, 14 Sept. 2016, www.-goodtherapy.org/blog/8-dimensions-of-wellness-where-do-you-fit-in-0527164. Accessed 10 Nov. 2022.

Hill, Catey. "This Common Behavior Is the No. 1 Predictor of Whether You'll Get Divorced." *MarketWatch*, 10 Jan. 2018, www.-marketwatch.com/story/this-common-behavior-is-the-no-1-predictor-of-whether-youll-get-divorced-2018-01-10.

Hughes, Kris. "25 of the Best Planning Quotes."
ProjectManager.com, 4 Oct. 2018, www.projectmanager.-com/blog/planning-quotes. Accessed 10 Nov. 2022.

Jarrett, Christian. "Is It Better to Be like Your Partner?" *Bbc.com*, BBC Future, 2018, www.bbc.com/future/article/20181011-are-rela-tionships-better-if-partners-are-more-similar. Accessed 10 Nov. 2022.

"Kevyn Aucoin Quotes." *BrainyQuote*, www.brainyquote.-com/quotes/kevyn_aucoin_358534. Accessed 10 Nov. 2022.

Korbin, Mel. "Promoting Wellness for Better Behavioral and

Physical Health." *SAMHSA*, mfpcc.samhsa.gov/ENewsArti-
cles/Article12b_2017.aspx. Accessed 9 Nov. 2022.

LAWYER, SAMANTHA. "80 Best Spiritual Quotes That Will
Give You Wisdom about Your Life's Journey." *Woman's Day*, 2
May 2022, www.womansday.com/life/a39788446/spiritual-quotes/.
Accessed 10 Nov. 2022.

"Lucius Annaeus Seneca Quotes." *BrainyQuote*,
www.brainyquote.com/quotes/lucius_annaeus_seneca_100585.
Accessed 10 Nov. 2022.

*Maddox Shaw, A. M.M., Rhoades, G. K., Allen, E. S., Stanley, S. M.,
& Markman, H. J.(2013). Predictors of extradyadic sexual involvement
in unmarried opposite-sex relationships. Journal of Sex Research, 50(6),
598 - 610.DOI:10.1080/00224499.2012.666816*

*Moran, Porcshe. "How Much Is a Homemaker Worth?" Investopedia, 13
Apr. 2020, www.investopedia.com/financial-edge/0112/how-much-is-a-
homemaker-worth.aspx.*

N/A, Nick, and Nick N/A. "These Hollywood Actors Are Living
Proof That Good Things Come in Small Packages." *SheKnows*,
29 June 2017, www.sheknows.com/entertainment/arti-
cles/952883/surprisingly-short-actors/. Accessed 10 Nov. 2022.

"Percentage of World Population over 6 Feet Tall." *Colonel-
height.com*, colonelheight.com/percentage-of-world-population-
over-6-feet-tall/. Accessed 5 Nov. 2022.

PK. "Average, Median, Top 1% Individual Income Percentiles
[2021] - DQYDJ." *DQYDJ – Don't Quit Your Day Job...*, 28 Sept.
2020, dqydj.com/average-median-top-individual-income-
percentiles/. Accessed 9 Nov. 2022.

---. "Income by Sex: Average, Median, 1%, and Calculator [2021]
– DQYDJ." *DQYDJ – Don't Quit Your Day Job...*, 1 Oct. 2020,
dqydj.com/income-by-sex/. Accessed 10 Nov. 2022.

SAMHSA. "CREATING a HEALTHIER LIFE a STEP-BY-
STEP GUIDE to WELLNESS." 2016.

Sander, Elizabeth (Libby) J., et al. "Psychological Perceptions
Matter: Developing the Reactions to the Physical Work Envi-

ronment Scale." *Building and Environment*, vol. 148, Jan. 2019, pp. 338–347, 10.1016/j.buildenv.2018.11.020.

---. "Psychological Perceptions Matter: Developing the Reactions to the Physical Work Environment Scale." *Building and Environment*, vol. 148, Jan. 2019, pp. 338–347, 10.1016/j.buildenv.2018.11.020.

"Social Wellness: Wellness at Northwestern - Northwestern University." *Www.northwestern.edu*, Northwestern University, www.northwestern.edu/wellness/8-dimensions/social-wellness.html. Accessed 10 Nov. 2022.

Stahl, Ashley. "Millennial's High Earning Years Have Arrived— Here's How to Prepare." *Forbes*, 10 Sept. 2021, www.forbes.com/sites/ashleystahl/2021/09/10/millennials-high-earning-years-have-arrived-heres-how-to-prepare/?sh=4b13daab4936. Accessed 10 Nov. 2022.

Strauss Cohen, Ilene. "How to Live an Emotionally Independent Life | Psychology Today." *Www.psychologytoday.com*, 4 Nov. 2019, www.psychologytoday.com/us/blog/your-emotional-meter/201911/how-live-emotionally-independent-life#:~:text=Emotional%20independence%20is%20a%20type. Accessed 12 Nov. 2022.

Theisen, Angela. "Is a Sense of Belonging Important?" *Www.mayoclinichealthsystem.org*, Mayo Clinic, 8 Mar. 2019, www.mayoclinichealthsystem.org/hometown-health/speaking-of-health/is-having-a-sense-of-belonging-important. Accessed 10 Nov. 2022.

Thompson, Karl. "What Percentage of Your Life Will You Spend at Work?" *ReviseSociology*, 16 Aug. 2016, revisesociology.com/2016/08/16/percentage-life-work/. Accessed 10 Nov. 2022.

"YouTuber Fixed Elon Musk Biggest Problem." *Www.youtube.com*, Money tips, www.youtube.com/shorts/nK-Zj2znTso.

Made in the USA
Las Vegas, NV
02 March 2024

86606810R00118